T0273469

WHAT OTHERS ARE SAYING
ABOUT *DEEP FAITH*

After years of leadership in God's Kingdom I am done listening to the voices of doubt, fear and discouragement! Why is the Church filled with these kinds of voices? I need friends with strong faith; deep faith. Rob Reimer is such a friend. His books and his life always inspire me to trust God for more. Time with Rob raises my faith level. *Deep Faith* will help you silence the voices of doubt, fear and discouragement and help you tune your ear to the voice of the One who declares, "with God all things are possible."

—**DR. RON WALBORN**, *Vice President of Nyack College and Dean of Alliance Theological Seminary*

Authentic faith has remained a challenging quest of both insightful and passion people for centuries. With updated insights, Deep Faith addresses both the challenges and the payoffs of a life that pursues an existence beyond the normal. Rob Reimer, a trusted friend and colleague, not only writes it well, but he also lives it well. If you want to go to the next level in life or in faith, this book will serve as a significant tool to guide you on your quest.

—**DR. MARTIN SANDERS**, *President & Founder, Global Leadership, Inc. and Director of the Doctor of Ministry Program at Alliance Theological Seminary*

Among Christian authors, living or dead, there are so few like Rob. His passion for spiritual renewal leaps off every page of *Deep Faith*. His hunger for God's manifest presence is all-consuming and contagious. Rob writes about what he knows and Who he knows, his pen a pointer to the greatness and glory of God. At a time when so many are tempted to discount the miraculous, to trivialize the supernatural, Rob moves in the opposite direction. He upholds the view expressed in the pages of Scripture and embraced by Christians the world over: God has a long history of responding in miraculous ways to men and women of faith. If you long to be more connected to the Source, to drink deeply at the Wellspring of abundant life, to live in a way that defies convention, then this is the book for you. You will not find a more trustworthy guide into the realm of deep faith than my friend, Rob Reimer.

—TOM WARD, *Advocacy Global*

Deep Faith is yet another seminal work by Rob Reimer for Christians desiring to break free of cultural Christianity and deepen their faith. Rob's personal testimony, transparency in describing his own battles to expand his faith, and his Biblical teaching on the subject is refreshing and challenging. For all called to serve as soldiers on the Kingdom's front lines, this book imparts important truths and principles needed today.

—CHAPLAIN (LIEUTENANT COLONEL) DAVID BOWLUS, *U.S. Army Chaplain*

In recent years the role of the Holy Spirit in the believers life has received growing attention around the Christian world. In this book Rob Reimer has brought Biblical patterns, applicable principles and personal insights into the Holy Spirit's work in the life of the believer. He writes as one who has pursued and wrestled with God and found keys to a deeper faith walk. This work challenges and encourages us to that deeper journey—for the partisan, pupil, preacher or proclaimer of faith in Christ.

—REV. KEN GRAHAM, *President, Christian and Missionary Alliance of Australia*

In this post-truth era, many ask, "What is faith?" Beneath this question is a deep longing to know how to live the Christian life with power. So many of us have inherited models that cannot sustain us neither do they help us to stand tall in the face of prevailing culture. Rob reminds us that faith is as accessible as letting go of our guardrails of worldly security to walk with open hands, confident in the faith that Christ so freely gives. Rob writes as he teaches: his words convey a sense of gravitas, coming as they do from a life that is wholly devoted to living faith with integrity.

—**TANIA WATSON,** *Executive Minister, Churches of Christ in Western Australia Inc.*

This is a powerful, challenging and uplifting read for the 21st century believer who desires to be the answer to the question—"can radical transformation be a steady part of my spiritual journey?" Dr. Reimer offers a wonderful mixture of anecdotal experiences and practical lessons from past heroes of the faith and from his own very dynamic experiences with God. "Deep Faith" is certainly one of those books that lives up to its promise.

—**BISHOP CARLTON T. BROWN,** *Pastor, Bethel Gospel Assembly, Harlem, NY*

Deep faith requires a deep work of God's refining power in our lives. It is not a momentary gift but a life time of cultivation that produces a risk-taking faith that releases the resources of Heaven. Rob Reimer invites us into the intimate places of his own soul journey to reveal the profound way in which God expands faith. He writes, "Faith releases the activity of Heaven on Earth. Faith is a conduit that carries the presence and power of God to our ordinary circumstances to produce extraordinary results for the glory of the Father." What makes this book so powerful is the clear premise that deep faith can only grow in the soil of profound humility. The posture of "empty hands" and "desperate longing" for the presence of Jesus becomes the atmosphere in which faith moves from hope to certainty. This book is a game changer for anyone who is passionate about moving from a mere observer of God's reviving presence to an active participant in it.

—**DAVID HEARN**, *President, Christian and Missionary Alliance, Canada*

In *Deep Faith* Rob invites the reader to pursue an active, faith-filled, fully-focused journey with Jesus. There are no quick fixes or "feel good Christianity" here. This is the real stuff. Faith can contain disappointment and always involves risk but… the other side of faith is power, encounter, freedom, and the very presence of Jesus. Bottom line, this book makes me want to go after Jesus with more intensity and creates more certainty that He is actually at work and wants to involve us in it!

—**DR. TIM MEIER**, *Director of Envision*

Rob Reimer goes deep. He is a deep diver, and in *Deep Faith* he takes those of us who prefer to splash around in the shallows with him. We see that God loves to be trusted and has an amazing life He wants to give us if we'll just go deep. If you're feeling becalmed in life, you owe it to yourself to take a deep dive and read this book.

—**SETH BARNES**, *Founder and President, Adventures in Missions*

Deep Faith

Developing Faith That
Releases the Power of God

Dr. Rob Reimer

Carpenter's Son Publishing

Published by Carpenter's Son Publishing, Franklin, Tennessee

Published in association with Larry Carpenter of
Christian Book Services, LLC
www.christianbookservices.com

Edited by Robert Irvin

Cover Design by John Pepe

Interior Layout Design by Suzanne Lawing

Printed in the United States of America

978-1-942587-88-0

ACKNOWLEDGEMENTS

We came into the world with nothing, and we will take nothing with us when we leave—in between, we owe a lot of people a debt of gratitude.

To my family: Jen, Danielle, Courtney, Darcy and Craig—much of my writing, speaking, and traveling takes something away from you, but you give cheerfully and love graciously. And I am grateful. Thanks for all of the laughs, joy, games, fun, love, and energy you bring into my life. I can't imagine life without you. You are all really good people that would make any good man proud, and I'm lucky to call you my own.

To the church family that I have loved and pastored for so long: I have learned much of the lessons in this book on the frontlines of church ministry at South Shore Community Church. I have labored alongside of you for 22 years, and now this year, as I take my leave from the pastorate and transition into a full-time professorship, I leave with deep love in my heart for you and much gratitude. For all your years of service to the King and his Kingdom, for all your graciousness with my shortcomings and my traveling, for all your sacrifices for the cause and for all your commitment to his mission in the world: I am grateful.

To great saints who have gone before me and who have inspired my faith—I am grateful. No one's life has inspired my faith more than George Muller. I would not be where I am today without the prodding of this man's life of faith. In all the books I've read, and all the Saints I've met, I have never seen anyone who has demonstrated the consistent certain faith of George Muller. I am so grateful.

To Andi Long: Again! Thank you! Every writer ought to

have someone like you in their life. You are a gift from God. Thank you for editing, shaping, supporting and occasionally cajoling me along. I am grateful for your brilliant mind, your gracious spirit, and your relentless pursuit of excellence.

To all of you who have read my previous books, and are fellow sojourners on this spiritual pilgrimage, thank you. Thanks to those of you who have written to me, sent me Tweets, Facebook messages, or spoken to me over the years about how the books have impacted your intimacy and walk with Jesus. That's why I write.

To Jesus. Empty hands. That's all I have apart from you. Empty hands. I supply the empty hands and the willing heart, and you supply everything else. You alone are worthy; you alone deserve the glory.

DEDICATION

I dedicate this book to my wife, Jennifer. Outside of my decision to follow Jesus, marrying you is the best decision I ever made in my life!

I think back to our wedding day quite often. Most people cut the cake and either smash it in their partner's face or just feed them very gently. But not you. You acted like you were going to feed me, and as I opened my mouth to take it, in one stealthy move you took it back and ate it yourself. I can still see the playful smile on your face. I still look back on that memory with fondness. Who else would do that? So clever, fun, playful, witty. No wonder I adore you.

Marriage hasn't always been easy. We have had some tough spots along the way, but it has always been worth it. Your honesty and magnanimity have inspired me to mature through conflict, to turn from wrongdoing and to become a better man. Your cheerful disposition and good humor have broken through the storm clouds of my bad mood like a ray of sunshine on more occasions than I can recall. Your winsome smile, keen wit, and infectious laughter have been a source of consistent joy to my soul and warmth to my heart. Your tender heart and gentle tears have softened me when I had hardened, healed me when my heart was hurt, recalled me to Jesus when I had wandered, and broke me when I had been the painful cause of their flow. Your honesty and guileless ways have called the best out of me and cultivated the best in me. Your ability to laugh at yourself has caused me to take myself less seriously and heartened me to greater heights of honesty and greater depths of humility.

Sometimes I ask people what they would do differently if they could do life over. I am always amazed at the alarmingly high percentage of people who say, "Nothing." How could you live life and not learn anything? I would change a lot of things if I could. I've had a good life, and we have had a happy marriage, but I would change things to make them better. Almost every regret I have in life centers on you. I wish I would have been an even better husband; I wish I would have been more loving, more tender, more attentive, more giving, more gracious, more helpful, and less selfish, less angry, less preoccupied, less impatient and less opinionated. Even as I write these words, tears slide down my cheeks because of my tender affections for you. I wish I had done things differently, and loved you more like Jesus loved the church, because you deserve it. I once had a dream that I had married someone else. I woke up sobbing. It would have been my greatest regret of all. Thank God I don't live with that regret! I have so many things to be grateful for in life. But every day at the top of my list is this: God gave me you.

The pain of this world has always pierced your heart. Yet somehow or other sharing life with you has made the world seem less harsh to me. You see the pain, but you carry healing to others. You feel the harshness but carry tenderness. You make the world a better place. It's a beautiful thing to watch.

Faith has never come easy to you. It has been a struggle, yet you are hopeful, cheerful, delightful, and admirable. So many who struggle for deep faith become embattled and embittered, but not you. All people are born sinners; that's why we need Jesus. But some people seem to have a nobler, purer soul than others. You are one of those rare souls marked by such nobility and beauty.

It is no wonder why we are twenty seven years into marriage and you are still the woman of my dreams. You are still the first person with whom I would choose to do anything, be anywhere, tell anything, share anything. When I receive good news, you are the person I can't wait to tell. When something painful happens, you are the person I want to see. When I am anywhere in this beautiful world all alone admiring God's creation, my first thought is always, "I wish Jen were here with me." When I think of someone I admire, you are the first person that comes to my mind.

When we get to Heaven, you can have your own mansion, but I hope I get to live next door because I can't imagine doing eternity without you by my side. We have gotten along well; we have been a good team. We have raised four beautiful children—to whom you have been an exceptional mother, and their development is in large part a credit to your diligent efforts. The children came and filled our house with joy, but now they are leaving the nest. Friends come and go. But, through it all, you remain.

John Maxwell once said that success is when the people who know you the best love you the most. If that is true, you may be the most successful person I know.

With all my heart,
Your loving husband

CONTENTS

"Faith sees the invisible, believes the unbelievable, and receives the impossible."

– Corrie ten Boom

Greater Things

In May 2016 I stood before the graduating class at Alliance Theological Seminary (ATS), where I teach. Each professor is given approximately twenty-five words to leave with that year's class of graduating masters and doctoral students. Twenty-five final words to make an impact, leave an impression, make a mark.

When it was my turn to speak, I asked the students to hold up empty hands. Hundreds of students stood before me in their caps and gowns, with their achievements and degrees, and in unison held up empty hands. I waited a moment in silence as we all stood together in the solidarity of our emptiness, and then I spoke from the heart.

"That's what you have apart from Jesus. Nothing. Apart from Jesus, we can do nothing. It's all about Jesus. Pursue his face, not his hands. Listen to his voice. Love Him first of all. Obey Him in all. Follow Him above all. Because apart from Him . . . " I held up my empty hands as all the students lifted their empty hands once again.

We stood together with our empty hands in a moment of silence, reminding us of our great need for Jesus' presence and power in our lives. I walked from the platform, and the students erupted in cheers.

Empty hands. That's what I have apart from Jesus; I have nothing. It's not just a slogan or some sort of gimmick. It is a physical reminder of a spiritual reality; it is a visible expression of the invisible condition of the soul.

Jesus said it: "I am the vine; you are the branches. If you remain in me, and I in you, you will bear much fruit; apart from me you can do nothing" (John 15:5). Only Jesus can save a lost and sin-stained human being. Only Jesus can change a life. Only Jesus can heal a broken heart and restore a damaged soul. Only Jesus can heal the sick. Only Jesus can set the captives free and deliver the oppressed. Only Jesus can impart the peace of Heaven to the anxious of heart, and only Jesus can fill the despairing with hope once again.

We need Jesus to do the works of the Kingdom of God, and that is precisely what Jesus wants to do through us. Jesus said, "Very truly I tell you, all who have faith in me will do the works I have been doing, and they will do even greater things than these, because I am going to the Father. And I will do whatever you ask in my name, so that the Father may be glorified in the Son. You may ask me for anything in my name, and I will do it" (John 14:12-14, TNIV).

This is one of my all-time favorite passages of Scripture, and one of the most astounding in the Bible. Many times we read the Bible but don't really believe what it says; we find ways to explain it away so we can feel more comfortable with our spiritual lack. But take this passage for what it says, just for a moment. Jesus promises that "all who have faith in me will do the works that I have been doing."

This is the content of the promise: We can do the works Jesus has been doing. Jesus healed the sick, cast out demons, saved the lost, and set the captives free. Jesus did miracles that defied the laws of nature and manifested the presence and power of God. This is the work of the Kingdom that He promised we would participate in.

This is the scope of the promise: It is for *all*. "All who have faith in me . . . " That included the disciples, and we know that they went on to live a supernatural life filled with the miraculous activity of the Kingdom—just read the book of Acts. And it includes you and me. We too have been called to live this Kingdom lifestyle by the power of the Spirit.

But this is the condition of the promise: It is dependent on our faith in Jesus. He says, "All who have faith in me." Here is the truth: Sometimes our faith is insufficient to see the works of the Kingdom. This isn't to blame or shame anyone. I am not interested in assigning blame, but I am interested in exploring the *potency of faith*. And there is hope for all of us, no matter what our current level of experience is, because faith can be developed.

Jesus starts this passage in John 14:12 with a formulaic expression, "Very truly I tell you." Jesus only uses this expression when He is about to unveil a truth that requires revelation to understand; He only uses this double verification ("very truly," literally, "truly truly") when He is about to lay a truth on us that is so outrageous that He knows our first instinct will be to dismiss it out of hand because it seems so utterly incomprehensible that there must be an alternative meaning (to his otherwise plain words)! He lays this double truth on us to make us pause and wrestle, honestly, with the weight of what He is saying, with the human impossibilities that the Divine Presence makes possible.

Our natural tendency is to take a myopic view of our circumstances, one that leaves us limited to our own perspective and resources. So often we cannot see beyond the boundary of our human potential. We limit ourselves to what we can do with our gifts and our best efforts. Jesus throws out a "very truly" in this passage to call us to suspend our limited vision, to take a wide-angle view that includes God's supernatural capacity to surpass all our natural limitations through the presence and power of his Holy Spirit.

We cannot possibly grasp the outlandish promises of God, nor the mysteries of the Kingdom, with our human minds. We need the revelation of the Holy Spirit. So, because He knows that we will automatically balk at the extraordinary nature of the promise, He backs it up with a double truly. "Truly truly"—or, as the NIV says, "Very truly." *Very truly*, we can do the things Jesus did.

Pause. Ask yourself: Is that true of my life? Is my life characterized by the works of the Kingdom? According to Jesus, very truly, all who have faith in Him ought to be doing the works of the Kingdom.

> According to Jesus, very truly, all who have faith in Him ought to be doing the works of the Kingdom.

As if that weren't mind-blowing enough, Jesus doesn't stop there. He goes on to stretch the limits of our credulity by promising that we can do "greater things than these." It is an utterly remarkable promise.

Sometimes we read the Bible with such familiarity that we no longer allow it to create a dissonance in our inner being, one that will make us cry out to God. There are passages that ought to make us throw ourselves down before God and cry out to Him for what only He can do, and this is one of those! If reading this passage doesn't incite you to humbly cast yourself at the feet of Jesus, then you are probably in danger of simply explaining it away. If reading this passage doesn't inspire you to humbly cry out for more, you are likely already settling for less. Feeling the dissonance is an essential first step to the development of faith.

Jesus doesn't necessarily mean we will do greater things

in quality, but greater in quantity. There are now more of us, and He is going to the Father so He can release the Spirit to abide in us. This is the key: the Holy Spirit is the great multiplier. God sent the Spirit to us to multiply the works of the Kingdom through us. The Father planned to use us to advance his Kingdom works, because He is on a search-and-rescue mission to redeem humanity. He knew we could not fulfill this mission without his presence, so He sent us the Holy Spirit. He dwells in us, and when we walk in the fullness of the Spirit, we can do the things that Jesus has been doing. It's not because we have any magical abilities, but because the Spirit of God is now in us and with us, and because God is passionate about his mission.

We can multiply the works of the Kingdom through the power of the Spirit. But it has to be about God and his mission to redeem humanity. It can't be about us. Too often we make it too much about us, and therefore, too often we see too little of his Kingdom.

This whole remarkable promise is contingent upon faith. God's part is to give us the promise, to send the Spirit, and to provide the power necessary for success on this King's mission. Our part is faith. "Very truly I tell you, all who have faith in me will do the works I have been doing." We have to humbly believe and receive from the King's hands.

There are things that God wants to happen in the Kingdom that cannot happen without faith. There are things that are currently not happening in the Kingdom because of the low level of our faith. There are promises in Heaven that God wants to release in power on Earth, but they cannot be released without faith. There are miracles that God wants to do in our lives that cannot be done without faith. There are answers to prayer that God wants to unleash in our midst that cannot be unleashed without faith. There are works of the Kingdom that God wants to accomplish on this planet that cannot be accomplished unless the people of God develop deeper faith. There are things right now that cannot be done because of our lack of faith—but that can be done in the future if we develop faith.

Faith is not static; it is dynamic. We can and must take an intentional path toward growing and developing our faith if we want to see the works of the Kingdom in greater measure, for the glory of the King, and for the sake of his mission in the world.

Jesus went on to say, "I will do whatever you ask in my name, so that the Father may be glorified in the Son. You may ask me for anything in my name, and I will do it" (John 14: 13, 14). We have to ask in Jesus' name. That is, in accordance with the heart and mind of Christ. This isn't magic; it isn't easy believe-ism. It's not a name-it-and-claim-it teaching. Jesus wasn't teaching that we could ask for more money to spend on our own selfish desires—as if we just have to name what we want, and believe, and we can claim it for ourselves. Jesus is saying that if we want to advance his Kingdom, for his glory, in his name, we can do the works He was doing because He was going to the Father and sending the Spirit. But we must have faith. Faith releases the activity of Heaven on Earth. Faith is a conduit that carries the presence and power of God to our ordinary circumstances to produce extraordinary results for the glory of the Father.

When I first started ministry, I read passages like this one, and I believed at some level. While I believed I would see the works of the Kingdom, the reality was that I saw far less Kingdom activity than I anticipated. I prayed for lots of sick people, but only a few were healed. I prayed for many people to be filled with the Holy Spirit, but only a few were truly, visibly, and demonstrably filled. I prayed for many of the works of Jesus to take place, but few did. I didn't understand why, but I continued believing there was more than what I was experiencing. I wasn't satisfied with the little I experienced, and I wasn't willing to settle for less than what I read in Scripture.

When what we read in Scripture doesn't match up with our own experience, we only have two options: Either we lower the expectations of Scripture to explain away our impotent experience, or we intentionally seek to elevate our experience and our faith to come into alignment with Scripture. To elevate our experience, we must feel the uncomfortable tension between what the Bible says and what we are experiencing. We must see the gap and feel holy discontent over it, and we must decide that we are going to do our part to close the gap. It is in this gap that faith has the potential to be developed. It is in this tension that the resolve is formed that is necessary to develop our faith.

* * * * * * *

There is one church service that stands out to me as a defining moment in my early journey toward faith. It clearly highlighted the importance of faith to me, more so than any other service we held. I was scheduled to preach on healing from James 5:13-16 one Sunday morning. I wrote my talk, as usual, on a Monday; I prayed over it and practiced it during the week. On Sunday morning I woke up and was praying about the service, and as I waited on God, I felt a prompting of the Spirit stirring in my soul: "Preach the message exactly as you have prepared it. But at the end of the message just add this sentence: 'The Lord led me to preach on this passage this morning because He wants to heal some people today.'"

I balked. "I don't know, Lord. I need this to be confirmed; I can't stand up and say that. What if I'm wrong? What if that isn't really you? What if that is just my desire? What if no one gets healed? *I'm* the one who looks like a fool. I need to know that it is really you speaking this to me." We must always pay attention to our self-talk: too often we talk ourselves out of faith. I waited on God, but I heard nothing else. God does not always make faith easy, nor does He always confirm everything so clearly that we don't need to trust. Often when God goes silent it is because He has already told you what He wants you to do, and now He is waiting on you to do it.

Faith is often fraught with knee-knocking risk and the undeniable possibility of real-world failure. I debated whether to add that sentence to the end of my talk all that morning through the service. I'd be lying if I told you that this Sunday morning was a peaceful Sunday morning for me. I was wrestling with God, searching for confirmation, struggling with the possibilities of a disastrous risk all through the worship.

After worship I stood up and delivered the talk just as planned, and then came the crucial moment of decision. Would I stick my neck out on this prompting and risk more than I was comfortable with?

I took the risk. I told the congregation what happened that morning as I prepared and prayed, that the Lord told me that He led me to give this talk today because He wanted to heal people. It was an ordinary Sunday morning with a fairly usual talk—until that moment. As I released that word, prompted by the Spirit, it created a palpable atmosphere of faith in the room.

Many responded and came forward to be anointed with oil and receive prayer for healing. We had more than a dozen people healed that morning. John came that morning heavily medicated because he was in severe back pain. He was scheduled for back surgery, but he came forward for prayer. As the prayer team laid hands on him and prayed, he felt heat in his back, and all the back pain left his body. He went home and threw away the medication he was on and canceled the back surgery. John lived many more years before he went on to Heaven—but he never needed back surgery.

Janis was sick to her stomach. Every time she ate, she threw up, but it wasn't a virus. She had scheduled an appointment with her doctor for the next day because it had gone on for so long. As she was sitting there listening to the talk, she debated whether she should come forward for prayer, reasoning to herself that there were so many others there with more pressing problems. While she was contemplating this, the power of the Spirit of God entered her shoulder, traveled down to her stomach, and instantly healed her. She went home to eat, and all her stomach problems were cured.

One person came forward for prayer because she suffered from migraine headaches. She even had one that morning. While she was standing in line for prayer, God healed her, and the migraine lifted.

It was a morning to be remembered, one in which the Kingdom of Heaven invaded Earth, and divine healing was released in our midst.

We had other healing services before this one, but never with this result, where so many people were healed. What was the difference this time? What happened? I think it would be easy to chalk this up to the sovereignty of God, and I honor and revere God's sovereignty. But I think there was a human component to this partnership in the Kingdom as well: Faith. On this occasion the Lord prompted me to take a risk and say something that would provoke faith in the hearts of his people so He could release his healing power. I had to believe this nudging was from God, and I had to be willing to risk looking like a fool in order to step out in faith and provoke faith in others. I did my part, the people responded in faith for their part, and the Lord healed—doing what only God can do. There is often a divine partnership between the faith of God's people and the release of God's power.

Imagine if "all who have faith" in Jesus were doing the works of the Kingdom because they developed the deep faith necessary to see the works of the Kingdom. Imagine the power of God that would be released in the world on the King's mission, for the King's glory. Imagine the people who would be saved, the lives that would be changed, the captives that would be freed, the bodies that would be healed, the miracles that would be produced, the poor that would be cared for, the damaged souls that would be restored—all for the glory of Christ.

Times have changed, but Jesus hasn't. "Jesus Christ is the same yesterday and today and forever" (Hebrews 13:8). He still has the power to do the things He did, but do we have the faith to believe Him for the works of the Kingdom?

I have a confession to make: My faith often wobbles. I am not writing this book because I have this figured out. I am writing this book because I think we need to develop deep faith, and I am a fellow sojourner on this path. I am writing this book with the deep conviction that if we develop faith, there will be a greater release of the works of the Kingdom in our midst.

There are times I have limited the activity of God in and around me because of my lack of faith. There are times I've had a promise from God, and I believed it fervently for a season, only to struggle to believe it when the promise was delayed in coming. I wobbled. There are times I have believed God strongly in one area while doubting God just as strongly in another.

But I can also tell you that my faith has developed over the years. Faith is developmental. I have faith for things today that I did not have faith for ten years ago, and I see the difference in the works of the Kingdom. In some areas that difference is dramatic, while in other areas I am still making only small strides. *We can grow, expand, strengthen, and develop our faith.* If our faith develops, we can believe God for things tomorrow that we do not believe God for today, and we can see more of the works of the Kingdom for the glory of Christ.

I am in a season of my life in which I am holding on to some promises from God that are yet to be fulfilled. I have been hanging on to some of them for more than a decade. There have been times over this last decade where the promises burned bright and passionate in my soul; my faith was red hot. And there have been times where I have struggled to my core to believe God for these promises, and my faith felt like a candle flickering in the wind. At my darkest times I have doubted, I have been discouraged, I have felt defeated, and I have deliberated throwing in the towel on some of these promises. But I have held on to them through it all. I have not been passively waiting for something to happen. I have been actively engaged in strengthening my faith.

I went through the deepest valley of testing I ever passed through as I prayed through these promises. And then I had to navigate through the treacherous valley of a dark night of the soul, where the presence of God was absent for the first time in my life. In the midst of that dark valley and that dark night, I had less faith than I ever had in my entire spiritual journey. Yet somehow, by the mysterious work of a loving Father, a purging occurred through the testing and through the dark night that left me with a deeper faith. It was a deep inner work of the Spirit that I cooperated with—albeit with much failing, fear, and trepidation.

When I emerged on the other side of those dark places, I found out that I had been through a valley where my faith was developed, though it didn't feel like it was developing at the time. I began to see more works of the Kingdom than I had ever seen—and not by a small measure. This was a sizeable increase.

In this book I want to walk with you through the journey God led me on, to the principles of how faith is developed. I want to look at what faith is, how it works in God's Kingdom, and how to develop it so we can do the works of the Kingdom for the glory of Christ. I am convinced that there is much more to be experienced, more of the works of the Kingdom, but we can't experience more without developing our faith.

I am also convinced that in a pluralistic, syncretistic day and age where all deities are considered equal, only the unequal display of supernatural power will convince people of the supremacy of Christ. There is a lot at stake, well beyond our comfort and convenience—it is a critical time full of divine opportunities to reap an unparalleled harvest of souls. But we must develop our faith to lay hold of it.

It all starts with this: Hold up your empty hands. Literally. Hold them up and pause in silence for a moment. That is what you and I have apart from Jesus—nothing. Faith recognizes that we can do nothing of eternal consequence apart from Jesus. Faith turns to Him in utter dependence to see God do what only God can do. Faith recognizes that, apart from God, we will only ever see what our gifts and our efforts can accomplish. But with his presence and power, we can see the Kingdom come on Earth as it is in Heaven.

"Very truly I tell you, all who have faith in me will do the works I have been doing, and they will do even greater things than these."

Reflection Questions

1. Are you experiencing the works of the Kingdom in your life? To what extent? How are you experiencing them?

2. How has your faith developed through the years? In what areas of your life can you see the development of faith? What areas do you still need to see faith develop?

3. Do you allow yourself to feel dissonance between John 14:12 and your experience? How is this motivating you to seek God?

One:
The Importance of Faith

"A little faith will bring your soul to Heaven,
but a lot of faith will bring Heaven to your soul."

—Dwight L. Moody

One day I gave a sermon about the necessity of praying in faith. I talked about how God answers prayers that are prayed in faith; I was trying to inspire people to pray in this way. But after I gave the talk, a woman came up to me and asked, "Why do we have to exercise believing prayer? God knows what we need. Why doesn't He give us what we need? Why do we have to ask and believe God for it?"

She was clearly annoyed, because having to hold on in prayer, actively trusting God for answers, felt like too much work. I don't know what her circumstances were, or what she had been waiting on God for, but it was hard, and she wanted it to be easier; she wanted God to see her need and answer without her having to wait, pray, and trust. I understand where she was coming from, because I have felt spiritually parched while holding on in believing prayer in the midst of a drought of spiritual activity.

So why does God value faith so much? Why does He require us to persist in faith? An entire chapter in Hebrews is dedicated to people who persisted in faith, believing God against all odds, and enduring long seasons of difficult waiting. They are enshrined in the hall of faith because of their unyielding, stubborn, relentless faith. I may not understand all the reasons God has chosen to place so much value on faith, but of this I am certain: Faith really matters to God.

Amazed By Faith

It is hard to overestimate the importance of faith in the economy of God. Jesus often chides his disciples for their lack of faith. In the gospel of Matthew alone, Jesus speaks of "little faith" five times. Only twice does He speak of great faith in all of the gospels. Only two times in Scripture do we find that Jesus is amazed, and both times have to do with faith. Once He is amazed at a centurion for his *great* faith. Once He is amazed at the people of his own hometown because of their *lack* of faith. It would be a noble goal to live our life in such a way that Jesus would be amazed by our great faith. Let's take a look at these two incidents, where Jesus is amazed by someone's faith response.

The centurion came to Jesus on behalf of his servant, who was sick, paralyzed, and in terrible suffering. Jesus offered to come and heal the servant, but the centurion replied, "Lord, I do not deserve to have you come under my roof. But just say the word, and my servant will be healed. For I myself am a man under authority, with soldiers under me. I tell this one 'Go,' and he goes; and that one, 'Come,' and he comes. I say to my servant, 'Do this,' and he does it" (Matthew 8:8, 9).

The centurion understood authority—his understanding came from a life in the military. He had people who were above him in the army, and when they commanded him to do something, he obeyed. He had people who reported to him, and they responded obediently to his command. He did not need to be present to issue a command that was obeyed; he merely needed to issue the command. It could come in written form or spoken form, but it was to be obeyed. Obedience to the order of a commanding officer was assumed and expected, and disobedience had severe consequences.

It isn't difficult to understand where this man gained his insight into authority. What is amazing is that he applied this understanding of authority from the military world to Jesus in the spiritual world. From his understanding of military authority, he realized that Jesus had authority over sickness; this was a huge leap of logic, one no one else was making in Jesus' day. When Jesus spoke, sickness was vanquished. The Centurion reasoned that he didn't need Jesus to be present with his servant; he only needed Jesus to issue the command, the sickness would leave, and his servant would be made well. The centurion realized that disease would obey Jesus like he would obey his commander-in-chief—even from a distance.

Matthew records, "When Jesus heard this, he was amazed and said to those following him, 'Truly I tell you, I have not found anyone in Israel with such great faith.' . . . Then Jesus said to the centurion, 'Go! Let it be done just as you believed it would.' And his servant was healed at that moment" (Matthew 8:10, 13).

Faith moved the heart of Jesus to release the power of God. Many came to Jesus to be healed. But this man had an understanding of military authority that by faith he applied to Jesus' spiritual authority, and this keen insight of faith amazed Jesus. He is the only person recorded in the four gospels who amazes Jesus by his great faith. Pause and consider that. Hundreds of people interact with Jesus in the gospels; they follow Him, trust Him, obey Him, believe Him for miraculous healing, and yet exactly *one* amazes Jesus by his great faith. Imagine what God might be moved to do on our behalf if we could develop great faith. Imagine what extraordinary Kingdom exploits could be accomplished in the church if a generation arose who developed great faith.

Great faith begins with a keen understanding of the greatness of Jesus. Jesus' central message was about the Kingdom of God. He began his ministry announcing the Kingdom, He proclaimed it throughout his lifetime, and just before He ascended to Heaven, the last thing He talked to the disciples about was the Kingdom.

> Great faith begins with a keen understanding of the greatness of Jesus.

The Kingdom of God is the reversal of everything that went wrong in the world when sin entered the world; it is the restoration of the way God intended things to be before sin, the fall of humanity, and the brokenness of our planet. Jesus is the King of the Kingdom. And the Kingdom of Heaven is a superior reality to the fallen nature of Earth, because Heaven is eternal and Earth is temporal, and because Heaven is ruled by a superior King. The eternal realities of Heaven are superior to the temporal realities of Earth. It was the centurion's insight into King Jesus and his superior Kingdom that allowed him to have such great faith.

Our eyes are often focused on the devastation of our broken planet rather than the supremacy of our risen King. Only when our eyes can take in the grandeur of Jesus, and comprehend the superior reality of his Kingdom, will we begin to develop the kind of great faith that allows a word from Jesus to be spoken that alters reality.

The only other time we find Jesus amazed in the gospels is in Mark 6, and once again He is amazed over the issue of faith, but this time He is not amazed because of someone's spiritual perceptivity, but because of their spiritual dullness. Mark writes, "Jesus left there and went to his hometown, accompanied by his disciples. When the Sabbath came, he began to teach in the synagogue, and many who heard him were amazed" (Mark 6:1, 2).

It starts off well. People are amazed at the insightful teaching of Jesus. They are impressed, because Jesus taught not as one of the teachers of the day, but as a man with authority from God. He had unusual insight and revelation; this was obvious. But their amazement over Jesus' teaching sadly does not translate into faith.

Many people admire Jesus, and are impressed by Jesus, but do not have faith to believe Jesus for the works of the Kingdom. Many believers are inspired by his teaching and are devoted to Jesus, they receive the benefits of his saving work, but still it does not translate into faith that releases the power of God. His home crowd began questioning where the wisdom came from, asking, "Isn't this Mary's son and the brother of James, Joseph, Judas and Simon?" (Mark 6: 3). Mark concludes this sad story with these words: "He could not do any miracles there, except lay his hands on a few sick people and heal them. He was amazed at their lack of faith" (Mark 6:5, 6).

Don't miss this: Our lack of faith limits the activity of God in our midst. Jesus wasn't expecting this lack of faith, or He wouldn't have been amazed by it. When He started teaching, they were with Him; He felt the buzz and energy of the crowd, the excitement, the anticipation. But it didn't translate into faith that could produce the works of the Kingdom.

There are probably a host of reasons why the people didn't have faith. Maybe they hadn't seen any miracles in some time—if ever. Often when the church goes through a downturn in spiritual power, people begin to make theological reasons why God doesn't move with power anymore. They try to systematize their experience. Theologies that limit God's power are inconsistent with the Scripture we say we honor. Good theologies shouldn't systematize our experience and limit God; rather, they should systematize God's experience, exalt God and empower us to believe.

Maybe they struggled with envy. Their questions surely sound a bit sour: "Isn't this Mary's son? Aren't his brothers here among us?" Envy gets our eyes off of God and onto us, and it limits the activity of God in our lives. Envy quenches the Spirit and often causes us to question the fairness of God as we look at what others have that we are missing.

And maybe their familiarity with Jesus cost them spiritual eyes to see. It is often our perceived understanding of the Bible that keeps us from receiving fresh revelation from the Author Himself. We come to Scripture with our preconceived notions, and our often-entrenched theological positions, and we miss the revelation the Spirit has for us in the moment. It happened to the Pharisees. They spent their lives studying about the Messiah, and they missed his coming when He stood among them and revealed Himself. Our preconceived notions blind us to his prescient wisdom.

Whatever their reasons, the bottom line is they lacked the faith to see the activity of God in their midst. It saddened Jesus, and we find Him amazed for only the second time in the gospels.

And we learn an invaluable lesson from these two stories in which Jesus is amazed about the quality of people's faith: Faith moves the heart of Jesus to release the power of God, and lack of faith limits the activity of God in our midst.

Faith matters. It creates a spiritual atmosphere where God is moved to act. Therefore, we must learn how to develop the quality of our faith.

The Condition of Promise

God, in his sovereignty, has often tied his activity to our response to his spoken word and written Word. He has revealed promises through the whispers of his Spirit and through his Word that He longs to keep, but they are conditional on our responses. "For God so loved the world that he gave his one and only Son, that whoever believes in him shall not perish but have eternal life" (John 3:16). The promise of eternal life is conditional upon our faith—we must trust Jesus alone for our eternal life with God.

In John 15:5, Jesus says, "If you remain in me and I in you, you will bear much fruit." God wants us to bear fruit; He called us to Himself and appointed us to bear fruit, but the condition for our fruit-bearing is our abiding. Apart from Him we can do nothing. The command in the passage is not to bear fruit; fruit-bearing is a by-product of abiding. The command is to abide, and the condition of fruit-bearing is abiding.

Here's another conditional promise: "If we confess our sins, he is faithful and just and will forgive us our sins and purify us from all unrighteousness" (1 John 1:9). There is no sin that God cannot cleanse, except the sin that is not confessed. Jesus' blood is greater than all our sin, but unconfessed sin remains unaffected by the superior blood of Jesus, leaving us in bondage and shame. It is a conditional promise: God's desire is to forgive all, because He takes no pleasure in the death of even a wicked person, but his promise is conditioned on our response.

Over and over the Scriptures make promises available to those who will reach out in trusting dependence on God and receive them. The Father longs for a generation of faith-filled believers who will take Him at his Word and see the works of the Kingdom advanced so that the world will believe.

Leonard Ravenhill wrote, "One of these days some simple

soul will pick up the Book of God, read it, and believe it. Then the rest of us will be embarrassed. We have adopted the convenient theory that the Bible is a Book to be explained, whereas first and foremost it is a Book to be believed (and after that to be obeyed)."[1]

Jesus says in John 14:12, "Very truly I tell you, all who have faith in me will do the works I have been doing" (TNIV). The promise is for all, but it is contingent on faith.

We discussed that only twice does Jesus speak of great faith—we started with the story of the centurion. The only other time Jesus speaks of someone's great faith is in Matthew 15. This is the story about a Canaanite woman who came to Jesus because her daughter was being afflicted by an evil spirit and was suffering terribly. Jesus, uncharacteristically, wouldn't even answer her. When you see Jesus do something out of character, you must pause to ask why. In this case, I think he did it because of his disciples.

Notice that when Jesus doesn't answer her, "His disciples came to him and urged him, 'Send her away, for she keeps crying out after us.' He answered, 'I was sent only to the lost sheep of Israel'" (Matthew 15:23, 24).

Jesus had a mission from the Father. He was to go to the Israelites first, and then the disciples were to go to all the world with the gospel message. But I don't think that is the real reason Jesus doesn't answer her; after all, He answered the centurion, and he was not a Jewish man, so Jesus made exceptions to this general rule. I think the real reason is because of the prejudice of the disciples. They didn't like this people-group, and they sometimes mistakenly assumed that the people of God received the gifts of God because God favored them over others.

---

1 Ravenhill, Leonard. *Why Revival Tarries,* Bloomington, MN: Bethany House Publishers, 1987, p. 71

I suspect Jesus let her plead for help so his disciples would be forced to deal with her. The Jewish people called the Canaanites "dogs," and Jesus used this expression when he answered her pleadings: "It is not right to take the children's bread and toss it to the dogs" (Matthew 15:26). She boldly responded, "'Yes it is, Lord,' she said. 'Even the dogs eat the crumbs that fall from their master's table'" (verse 27). Boom! Jesus was thrilled: "Woman, you have great faith! Your request is granted" (verse 28).

I think Jesus saw this woman's desperation, and in it He saw the seeds of deep faith. He provoked a response of faith from her to give the disciples an example. Again, the promise is for "anyone who believes." She believed, and the works of the Kingdom were released against cultural norms and expectations. Desperation is often the platform of breakthrough. Desperation fuels humility, and humility results in great faith.

The disciples learned an invaluable lesson: the resources of God flow to all people who exercise faith. No one is excluded. They didn't receive gifts from God because they were superior, and others weren't excluded because they were inferior. Faith is the great equalizer; faith is the great qualifier. Faith opens doors and creates opportunities for accessing the power of God against all odds.

> Faith is the great equalizer; faith is the great qualifier. Faith opens doors and creates opportunities for accessing the power of God against all odds.

People who exercise deep faith are no longer limited to their own finite resources and abilities; they now access the infinite resources of God. Deep faith allows disadvantaged people to access the advantages of God. This woman was stuck behind a wall of prejudice that denied her access to Jesus, but her faith was a key that opened the doorway of privilege for her—not privilege with society, or victory over people's prejudices, but the privilege of God's favor that is reserved for all who believe.

Faith: A Conduit

Matthew tells another story about a man who was paralyzed (Matthew 9). His friends heard about Jesus and his healing power. They were so moved with compassion for their friend, and by their faith in Jesus' capacity to heal, that they took action. They carried their friend on a mat to where Jesus was. James tells us that faith without deeds is dead; faith must always move us into action. Matthew tells us that when they arrived, such a large crowd had gathered that they couldn't get into the house where Jesus was teaching.

These guys were not to be put off. They came on a mission, and no obstacle would keep them from their goal. They climbed up on the roof, made an opening, and lowered the man to Jesus.

"When Jesus saw their faith, he said to the man, 'Take heart, son; your sins are forgiven'" (Matthew 9:2). The man came for healing, but Jesus offered him forgiveness. Jesus saw past the man's broken body and into his tormented soul, and in response to faith Jesus offered the man the one thing he needed more than physical healing—the cleansing of his soul.

> Faith triggers a response from the heart of God, and it often leaves us with more than we bargained for, because God's heart is bigger than our capacity to see our need or ask aright.

Faith triggers a response from the heart of God, and it often leaves us with more than we bargained for, because God's heart is bigger than our capacity to see our need or ask aright. Faith opens the door for God to answer the yearnings of the heart and not simply the pleadings of the mouth.

The teachers who were there, however, were not pleased with this gesture. They knew theologically that only God could forgive sin. This is a simple principle: only the offended party can offer forgiveness. Forgiveness is a gift that is granted by the offended party; it is never deserved or earned. If a man cheats on his wife, he can come to me as a pastor and plead for forgiveness. I can offer him comfort. I can console him, but even if I say that I forgive him, it will not help him experience reconciliation with his wife. The only way he can be reconciled to his wife is if his wife offers him the gift of forgiveness.

How many gifts would he have to buy her before she has to offer him forgiveness? No amount of gifts would suffice; forgiveness is a *gift that is granted* by the offended party. Sin is a breach against God's law, and therefore an offense against God, and only God can grant the gift of forgiveness; it can never be earned or deserved. The teachers of the law knew this, and this is why they were angry with what Jesus said.

Jesus overstepped his bounds. Unless, of course, He was God, and then He could grant forgiveness. They were right about their theological understanding of forgiveness, but wrong about their conclusions concerning Jesus. Only a revelatory understanding of who Jesus is can access the deep faith that releases the resources of God.

Jesus knew what they were thinking, and He called them out for their evil thoughts. He challenged them by saying, "Which is easier: to say, 'Your sins are forgiven,' or to say, 'Get up and walk?'" (Matthew 9:5). Then Jesus said to the man, "Get up, take your mat and go home" (9:6). The man left restored in soul and body.

The conduit of this release of Heaven's resources was faith. Without faith, there is no bold action taken by the man and his friends. Without faith, there is no forgiveness and restoration. Without faith, there is no healing. It was when Jesus saw their faith that He released the resources of Heaven to meet their needs—both spiritual and physical.

On another occasion Jesus met a man named Jairus who was one of the synagogue leaders (Mark 5). His little girl was dying. I have four children, three daughters. I understand the desperation a parent feels in the face of a suffering child. Any good parent would take any measure necessary to help a suffering child.

Jairus needed a miracle worker, and he came to the one who was known for miracles. Unlike the centurion, who had an unusual insight into Jesus' authority over sickness, this man didn't tell Jesus just to speak the word. He didn't display that same great faith, but he did display sufficient faith. Jesus was not put off by being asked to come; He willingly accompanied the man to his house to cure his daughter.

As Jesus was walking with the man to his house, someone in the crowd touched Jesus. Jesus knew power had left Him, so He asked the crowd, "Who touched my clothes?" His disciples were baffled by this question because they saw the crowds pressing in all around Him—He was constantly being touched. But Jesus kept looking until the woman came forward and told her story.

She had been bleeding for twelve years and had spent all she had on doctors, but they could not cure her. She too was desperate, and she pressed through the crowds, snuck up on the one who had miracle-working power, reached out and touched Him, and she was healed.

Bleeding had left her with the social stigma of being declared unclean; this woman hoped to walk up, get healed, and slip away into the crowd. She had been humiliated enough publicly. But Jesus sought her out because He knew she didn't just need physical healing. She needed healing for her soul because of the shame she felt.

Jesus said to her, "Daughter, your faith has healed you. Go in peace and be freed from your suffering" (Mark 5:34). Once again, faith released the healing power of God for the healing of the body and soul. She didn't even ask Jesus for healing; she reached out in faith and grabbed hold of the Healer, and healing flowed to the faith that anchored her actions.

Unfortunately, as they continued to Jairus's house, word came that the little girl had died. Jesus overheard the messengers from Jairus's household, and yet He spoke these words to Jairus: "Don't be afraid; just believe."

> Circumstances threaten to extinguish the candle of our faith, and Jesus seeks to gently nurture the flame because He knows faith releases the resources of God.

I wonder how many times Jesus seeks to encourage our wobbling faith, knowing we are so close to a miracle, so close to an answered prayer, so close to a divine intervention. I wonder how many times we turn and walk away just before the breakthrough would come. Circumstances threaten to extinguish the candle of our faith, and Jesus seeks to gently nurture the flame because He knows faith releases the resources of God.

One of the great battles of nurturing our faith is to consistently look to Jesus instead of focusing on the circumstances that seem to deny his power. This is the importance of faith.

Jairus looked out of the grave and up to the one who was the Resurrection and the Life, and his weak faith was strengthened. The candle of Jairus's faith did not go out, and his little girl was raised from the dead. And in that moment, the eternal triumphed over the temporal, and the King of Heaven conquered the prince of the air—because Jesus responded to one man's unfaltering faith.

Over and over in the gospels, Jesus seeks to inspire, provoke, and encourage faith. Over and over He says things like "according to your faith it will be done to you," or, "don't be afraid; just believe," or "your faith has healed you." To some He says, "Your faith has saved you." To others He asks, "Where is your faith?" He chides people for "little faith" and commends people for active trust. When the disciples feel their faith failing, Jesus says, "If you have faith as small as a mustard seed, you can say to this mulberry tree, 'Be uprooted and planted in the sea,' and it will obey you." Another time He tells them, "Nothing is impossible for the one who believes." As the cross approaches, He tells Peter that He has prayed for him that his faith may not fail. And He tells them all, in John 14:12, "All who have faith in me will do the works that I have been doing, and they will do even greater things than these."

Faith has great capacity to release the power and resources of God. Faith moves the heart of God to intervene on behalf of his people. Faith is a key that unlocks the treasure house of God that is stocked with answered prayers. Faith is a conduit that carries the presence and power of God right into the midst of his people. Faith is a difference-maker, a future-shaper, a bondage-breaker, a Kingdom-mover.

> Faith is a conduit that carries the presence and power of God right into the midst of his people. Faith is a difference-maker, a future-shaper, a bondage-breaker, a Kingdom-mover.

Why Faith?

You may be reading and asking questions similar to those of the woman I mentioned at the beginning of the chapter: Why is faith so important? Why does God put so much stock in faith? God knows what we need before we ask, as Jesus said, so why doesn't He just answer without our needing persistent faith or without our even asking?

I think the fundamental answer comes down to trust. Trust is the foundation of all relationships. Trying to construct a building on a faulty foundation is futile. No matter how good the building materials, no matter how good the builder, the building is in jeopardy because the foundation is in question. We simply cannot build relational depth without trust—in any relationship. This is true of our relationship with a spouse, a child, or a friend. And it is true in our relationship with God.

Ultimately, God is seeking to establish a deep, trusting relationship with us. He wants us to trust Him—in all times, in all circumstances—because He is a good Father. It's easy to trust God when life is kind and good and all things are going our way. But it is a true test of our faith when life deals us a cruel hand.

Will we trust God when our marriage is in trouble and our kids are struggling and our financial future looks bleak? Will we trust God when our friends betray us, our boss fires us, or our health fails us? Will we trust God when we fervently seek his intervention and the answer is delayed in coming? Will we trust Him when the promises we have believed are but a distant memory and a heartbreaking hope?

The number one question on the heart of people for God is: Do you love me? God's answer is the incarnation of Jesus that led Him to a blood-stained cross, ultimately culminating in an empty tomb. God's answer is this: "I love you enough to send my Son to die for you. Now that I've proven my love, will you trust me?" This is the number one question on the heart of God for each one of us: Will *you* trust *Me*?

Will you trust God? No matter what? Will you trust God no matter who is for you or against you? Will you trust God no matter what life brings your way? Will you trust God no matter how long the promises are delayed?

God longs to be trusted because He is a good Father. He has proven his trustworthiness. Adam and Eve did not trust God enough to obey Him; they believed a lie that indicted Him with spurious motives, and they opted for distrust and disobedience. God longs to be trusted by you and me. We will not have opportunities to trust God in difficult, trying, painful, sin-tainted circumstances in Heaven. In Heaven, it will be easy to trust God. Only on Earth can we demonstrate great faith that triumphs over life's worst trials.

This is what the Father wants from you and me: Faith that believes He is fundamentally good, honorable, loving, righteous, and therefore worthy of all of our trust—no matter what comes our way. The depth of our intimacy with God cannot surpass the level of our trust in God. Our life of faith is a life of active trust in a righteous and loving Father who always has our best interest at heart.

At times, all of life seems to question that assertion, that fundamental truth about God's goodness, faithfulness, and trustworthiness. We must take full responsibility to develop, strengthen, and nurture our faith. Without faith, we are surely doomed to distrust and disobey. Without faith, we are certainly limited to what we can accomplish with our gifts and our endeavors. Without faith, trials and hardships will go unredeemed. Without faith, the church will be reduced to preaching and programs without the Presence and Power of God. Without faith, our hearts are bound to be injured by the difficulties of life and to become hard against God.

Faith matters to God because you demonstrate with your

active faith that God is good, that He is trustworthy. Faith matters to God because it honors Him for who He is, a loving Father who is utterly dependable. Faith matters to God because it takes into account an eternal perspective, not banking on the outcomes of everything in the present moment. Faith matters to God because it demonstrates that God is more important to us than getting what we want.

God is pleased with great faith; He is disappointed with little faith. He will love us whether our faith is great or small, but He will release the resources of Heaven to those who trust Him with deep faith. Faith moves the heart of God so deeply that it motivates Him to act on our behalf. Somehow or other, faith inspires God, moves God, touches the heart of God, and causes God to vouchsafe Himself, his power, and his privileges to us.

> God is pleased with great faith; He is disappointed with little faith. He will love us whether our faith is great or small, but He will release the resources of Heaven to those who trust Him with deep faith.

This kind of deep faith is developed over time. Little faith is easy come, easy go; little faith blows with the breeze and is scattered by the harsh winds of cruel circumstances. Little faith produces little results. But deep faith passes the test of time; deep faith has staying power and is rooted in the character, goodness, dependability, and trustworthiness of God. Deep faith is founded upon the love of God demonstrated on a cross. Deep faith takes into account our eternal citizenship in Heaven. This is the relational trust of a deep friendship that has been cultivated over many years. This is the faith we must develop.

My grandmother was a fearful woman. She was a woman

of great faith, but she clung to God in fear and trepidation quite frequently. When things didn't go well with the family, she was known to stay up all night and pray. It wasn't simply so that she could pray, it was also because her fear kept her from sleeping. She was known in times of tragedy not to eat; it wasn't simply so she could fast and pray, it was because she was so upset she couldn't eat. She was always able to pray through and get to a place of faith, but it didn't come easily for her, because her fear was great. Often our fear causes us to act in ways of unbelief, and it hinders the activity of God in our life. Fear is a tool of the enemy to keep us from the fullness of God.

When my grandmother died, I was reflecting on this fearful side. It was only then that I realized how deep her faith really was. It was harder for my grandmother to believe, to actively trust God, than it was for other people, for those who are less fearful than her by nature and life circumstances. She was so fearful, yet she learned to surrender to her good Father and trust Him no matter what. Though fear was always lurking in the shadows of her soul, she learned to hold on to the light of God in the darkest hours.

I went to visit my grandmother in the nursing home the year my grandfather died. He had been battling Alzheimer's disease for many years, and he was a mere shadow of his former self. He couldn't communicate well because the disease had robbed him of his once sharp mind. He sometimes was snappy, irritable, or behaved in ways that were inconsistent with the godly man he had been.

But my grandmother loved him, and in her fearfulness, she couldn't imagine life without him. My visit was on a cold, wintry day in January 2008. It was right around New Year's Day, a time of year that is supposed to be filled with hope and new beginnings. As I sat with my grandmother she said to me, "The Lord spoke to me and told me that this is going to be a hard year, a bad year, a difficult year for Pop."

The Lord, gracious as He is, was giving her a preview of the great loss that she was about to suffer. They had been married for more than seventy years; it was an immeasurably large loss for a woman of fearful disposition. She knew his time was drawing near to go to the Lord, and she was dreading it. But as I held her hand and prayed with her, she talked to me about the goodness and faithfulness of God. She talked about God's promises and provision. She talked to me about her hope in Heaven and eternal life. Her fear was great, but her trust in our good Father was greater still.

She had learned to trust Him through hardship and financial woes, through difficulties in marriage and kid troubles, through world wars and great depressions, through sickness and death. She trusted the whisper of his Spirit that warned her of this trying time to come; she trusted Him as the disease continued to ravage her husband throughout that year, and she trusted Him through the loss and grief. She trusted Him until her own time came, right up until her final breath. She trusted Him with her life; and in her death she trusted Him with her eternity. I saw her trust God for miracles, and He delivered. I saw her trust God in tragedies, and He was present and faithful still.

This is what deep faith looks and feels like. It isn't easy to come by; it isn't easy to hold onto. Deep faith still has a lot of warts and wounds and wobbles, but it keeps looking up to Jesus. It keeps trusting; it weighs all things in light of eternity, and it holds on to the goodness of God no matter what.

How do we develop deep faith that releases the power of God in our midst, and trusts Him through life's darkest hours? Let's go deeper in our next chapter.

Reflection Questions

1. Great faith is a rare and beautiful thing. Who have you known who has demonstrated unusually strong faith?

2. Our lack of faith limits the activities of God. What is it that undermines your faith? What can you do to combat that?

3. Monitor your self-talk. How does your self-talk, what runs through your mind unfiltered, help or hurt your faith?

4. The promises of God are conditional upon our responses. We must exercise faith. What promises of God's Word do you need to actively hold onto and trust God for in your life? In this precise moment of time?

5. How has Jesus tried to bolster your faltering faith? What tools has He used to strengthen your faith?

6. You will never be able to trust God in difficult, painful circumstances in Heaven. What are the difficult circumstances of your life that are providing you with an opportunity to demonstrate God-honoring faith? How can you respond?

Two:
The Faith Spectrum

*"Now faith is being sure of what we hope for
and certain of what we do not see."*

— Hebrews 11:1 (NIV, 1984)

"Faith takes God without any ifs."

— D.L. Moody

*"What now is faith? Nothing other than
the certainty that what God says is true."*

— Andrew Murray

Many years ago I had a revelation as I read Scripture, one
that launched me on a new journey to develop deep faith. I was
on my summer study break, and I read Matthew 10:1: "Jesus
called his twelve disciples to him and gave them authority to
drive out evil spirits and to heal every disease and sickness." I
had read these words hundreds of times before, but this time
fresh revelation from the Spirit came, and I was struck by the
incongruence of my faith.

I had been involved in deliverance ministries for many years, and I had complete confidence in casting out demons. I knew beyond a shadow of a doubt that every time I confronted a demonic spirit, when I commanded that spirit to depart, it had to go. If the person was willing to confess their sins and repent, I was certain the demons would depart. If that spirit resisted, it did not deter me, because I knew it had been defeated, and I knew it would leave—it was only a matter of time if the person was willing and I persisted and listened for the wisdom of the Spirit. I may have had to pray, fast, and persist, but in the end, the demon would have to leave.

While I had this deep faith in dealing with demonic spirits, my faith in praying for the sick was not even close to that level. Seldom had I ever prayed for a sick person with the same level of confidence. That summer day, as I read Jesus' words again, I was struck by the fact that there was something amiss in my faith. In this passage, Jesus gave his disciples authority to cast out demons and heal every disease. There was no distinction or differentiation in the text, but there certainly was in my mind and practice.

Luke's version tells us that Jesus gave them authority to cast out all demons and heal disease. So when you put the two Gospel accounts together, Jesus gave his disciples authority to cast out *all* demons and heal *all* disease. God had the same power sufficient for both situations, and He gave them the same authority to enforce his victory in both situations.

Yet in my own life, my faith was not the same for healing as it was for casting out demons, and the fruit that I saw was in direct proportion to the faith that I exercised. It was an undeniably startling revelation, and it was backed up with unmistakable evidence—I saw far greater results with deliverance than I did with healing.

This was a disquieting revelation. Revelation is not always comforting; quite often it is unsettling, as the Spirit seeks to settle his truth deep in our hearts. Think of it like breaking up fallow ground. If you are going to break up fallow ground, you are going to have to disturb the soil with a plow. But disturbing the hardened soil is what makes the soil open to receiving the seed and ultimately bearing fruit. When the Spirit brings conviction, He is unsettling the soil of our soul so we will bear more fruit. There was something deficient in my faith in this area of my life. Why could I take God at his word in one area and yet clearly struggle to believe Him in another?

Jesus said, "Very truly I tell you, all who have faith in me will do the works I have been doing, and they will do even greater things than these" (John 14:12).

Faith was the problem. I had some work to do to develop my faith.

The Faith Spectrum

Think about faith as a continuum. On the far left side of this spectrum, faith is very weak, and as you progress to the right side of the spectrum, faith grows stronger and deeper (see figure 1).

FIGURE 1

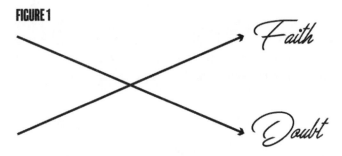

Notice too that there is room for doubt in the spectrum of faith. The opposite of faith is not doubt; the opposite of faith is unbelief. When we have weak faith, our doubt is high and our faith is low. But as we progress along the spectrum of faith, our faith gets higher and our doubt gets weaker. When we have unbelief, we have sin. We need to repent of sin. Unbelief isn't even on the spectrum of faith; it is outside the spectrum. Doubt isn't sin, it just hinders our faith. It still falls within the spectrum of faith, but the larger our doubt, the more ineffective our faith. When we

> Unbelief needs to be repented of; doubt needs to be dealt with by developing our faith.

have doubt, we need to develop faith. For example, you can have faith to believe Jesus will forgive your sins but remain in unbelief about Jesus' healing power. I know people who trust Christ as Savior but deny Jesus still heals. They have certainty over his saving work and unbelief about his healing power. Unbelief needs to be repented of; doubt needs to be dealt with by developing our faith.

But let's widen our view. Look at Figure 2: on the far left side of the continuum is hope. Sometimes our faith operates in the realm of hope, as in, "I hope something happens." We hope something will happen when we pray. We hope this sick person will be healed; we hope this person will come to faith in Christ and become a follower of Jesus; we hope this wandering friend will turn from their sin and return to God. *This form of hope-faith is a low level of faith, and it produces little spiritual result. It is intermingled with significant levels of doubt.*

FIGURE 2

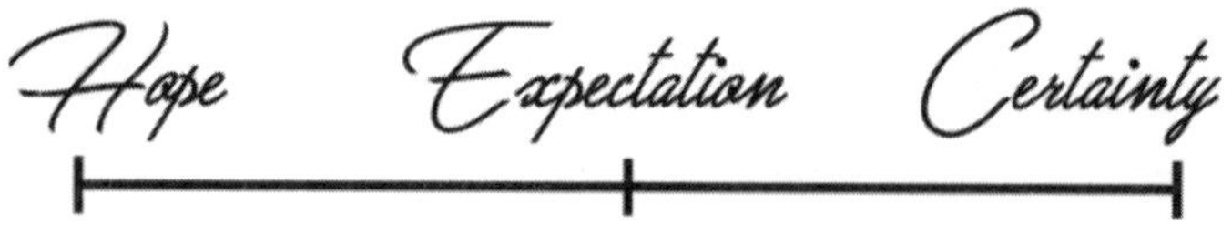

Hope   Expectation   Certainty

When I was praying for sick people in the early days, I

prayed with this sort of faith—I hoped something would happen, but I didn't really think anything would happen, and it seldom did. I believed God could heal the sick; at least theoretically and theologically, I believed it. I had a theology for healing, but I didn't have the personal depth of faith to have confidence in God to heal when I prayed. When I prayed for the sick, I prayed with *theological* belief in God's healing, but that was mixed with large levels of personal doubt that anything was going to happen. I was surprised if it did. This end of the spectrum is often a weak and sickly form of faith and needs to be strengthened and developed to see the works of the Kingdom with any consistency.

In the middle of the continuum is expectation. Now we pray with a degree of anticipation and expectation that God is going to answer our prayer. Our faith is still intermingled with doubt, but now our faith is much stronger and our doubt much weaker. We pray for a sick person, and we have the expectation that God can come and heal. We pray for a wandering friend to return to God, and we pray with fervency and passion because we anticipate the answer to our prayer. When we pray with eager expectation, we see more things happen. Prayer is more joyful and fruitful as a result, and our lives start to feel like a Kingdom adventure.

At the far right end of the spectrum is certainty. When we pray with certainty, we know the answer is coming. We don't hope, we don't expect; we know. Now our faith overpowers our doubt; doubt is barely noticeable at all. When I did deliverance ministry, I knew the demons would leave. It might require multiple sessions. It might require prayer and fasting and persistence. But I knew that, in the end, the demon would leave. There were times during a deliverance that a demonic spirit would demonstrate a powerful manifestation, and I would suddenly feel afraid and have moments of doubt, but I could take a deep breath, center my attention on Jesus and his victory, and doubt would flee, certainty would return, and the person would be set free.

When we pray with this level of certainty, stuff happens— the Kingdom comes on Earth as it is in Heaven, and the resources of Heaven are released. We see the works of the Kingdom.

Praying with Certainty

Jesus operated with this level of certainty. I know some people say, "Well, sure. But He was God." But when Jesus walked on the planet, He did everything out of his Spirit-anointed humanity, not from his divinity. In other words, He acted on Earth as a human who was dependent upon the Spirit—just like you and me.

Philippians 2:5-7: "In your relationships with one another, have the same mindset of Christ Jesus: Who, being in very nature God, did not consider equality with God something to be used to his own advantage; rather, he made himself nothing by taking the very nature of a servant, being made in human likeness."

Jesus made Himself nothing. Literally, He emptied Himself. What did He empty Himself of? He didn't empty Himself of his divinity; He was one hundred percent God and one hundred percent human. But He did lay aside his rights to use his divinity. He did not cease to be divine; He voluntarily chose to lay aside his right to use his divine attributes.

For example, Jesus laid aside his right to be omnipresent in his human body, and He limited himself to one place at a time. He laid aside his right to be omnipotent as a man, and He only did what the Father told Him to do in the power of the Spirit (which Jesus Himself emphasized; cf. John 5:19, 5:20, 8:28, 12:49). He limited his right to use his omniscience while in the flesh and chose to know only what He could observe and what the Spirit told Him. Jesus did not do his miracles because He was God. He did his miracles because He was in total alignment with his Father and the Spirit, and He did them by the power of the Spirit and in accordance with the will of the Father. He did miracles because of deep trust and unhindered relationship. We do miracles because Jesus is God and victorious, and we trust Him. "All who have faith in me will do the works that I have been doing." Just as Jesus said He could do nothing apart from the Father, He told us that, apart from Him, we can do nothing (John 15:5). Jesus modeled for us the way to live a Spirit-empowered, God-dependent, Kingdom-fruit-bearing life.

To grasp this concept, take a close look at the gospel of John. In John 4:34, Jesus met the woman at the well while the disciples were out getting lunch. When they returned, they suggested that He eat something, but Jesus said, "My food... is to do the will of him who sent me and to finish his work." Everywhere Jesus went, He asked one question: "What is the Father doing? What is the will of the Father in this situation?" His one objective was to find what the Father was up to and join Him in his work; this was his philosophy of ministry.

In John 5:19, Jesus said, "Very truly I tell you, the Son can do nothing by himself; he can do only what he sees his Father doing, because whatever the Father does the Son does also." In John 7:16, Jesus said, "My teaching is not my own. It comes from the one who sent me" (also, cf. John 8:28; 12:49, 50; 13:10; 13:24).

Jesus only did what the Father told Him to do, and He only said what the Father told Him to say. Everything He did, all of the works of the Kingdom He performed, He did in dependence on the Father, not in dependence on his divinity.

With that theological backdrop, consider John 11. Jesus went to see Lazarus, but before He even got there, He already knew—supernaturally, through the revelation of the Spirit—

that Lazarus was dead (John 11:11). Jesus also knew that He would raise him from the dead. He had absolute confidence in this. There was no shadow of doubt for Jesus.

When Jesus went to wake Lazarus from the grave, it wasn't a "Golly, I hope he gets up from the dead!" sort of prayer. This wasn't even in the middle of the spectrum: an eagerly expectant prayer. He was absolutely certain of the outcome.

He told Martha, "Your brother will rise again" (John 11:23). She thought He must be referring to the day of resurrection, but Jesus told her, "I am the resurrection and the life" (verse 25). He had absolute certainty about the outcome—this would not end in death. Jesus knew this was an assignment from the Father, and therefore He had absolute confidence in the outcome.

Jesus wept with Mary because his heart was moved with compassion, not because He was questioning the outcome. Then He went to the tomb and told them to remove the stone. Martha objected, concerned about the bad smell of the dead body. But Jesus simply said, "Did I not tell you that if you believe, you will see the glory of God?" (verse 40). He had no doubt; He lived in absolute certainty even in the face of death.

Then He prayed this prayer: "Father, I thank you that you have heard me. I knew that you always hear me, but I said this for the benefit of the people standing here, that they may believe that you sent me" (41-42). Absolute certainty: *I knew that you always hear me.* And with a command—"Lazarus, come out!"—the dead man came out of the grave. Just like Jesus knew he would.

Jesus was utterly dependent on the Father and totally confident of his coming victory. His absolute certainty produced the works of the Kingdom: a resurrection.

There have been times in your life, most likely, where you have operated with certainty in your faith. You, like me, have not likely lived there, but you have visited the neighborhood of certainty every now and then.

You may have prayed with certainty because you had a prompting of the Spirit, or a promise from the Word, or a deep inner assurance from the Father. You may have operated with certain faith for healing, or a miraculous breakthrough, or a financial provision.

One of the first times I visited the certainty side of the faith spectrum was when my uncle had a heart attack. The doctors had done everything humanly possible, but they called the family in and said, "There is nothing more we can do." They told us his heart was like hamburger meat and he was in the hands of God.

When I went to pray, the Spirit of God spoke to my inner being and said that my uncle would live and not die. I went in to pray for him, and I could see the fear in his face. My uncle had just come to faith, after living a life resistant to God. I looked him in the eye and said to him, "God told me that you will live and not die." And then I prayed a prayer of faith over him. He lived for many years after that, and his doctors affectionately referred to him as "the miracle man."

George Muller: A Life of Certainty

George Muller lived most of his life on this certainty side of the faith spectrum. If you have never read Muller's autobiography, or *Answers to Prayer,* by Muller, you should. I read *Answers to Prayer* annually to instruct me, inspire me, and develop my faith. Muller's life is filled with stories about how God miraculously provided for himself, a man who had complete confidence in God. Every time I read the accounts from Muller I am moved, motivated, and humbled.

George Muller prayed for the conversion of five of his friends. He prayed every day believing that these men would put their faith in Jesus. After five years, the first one came to Christ. After ten more years of prayer, two more came to

Christ. Once Muller spoke of praying for these five friends while he was in Chicago. He talked about those who had come to faith in Christ, and then he talked about the other two, for whom he was still persisting in prayer. Muller said, "I have prayed for two men by name every day for thirty-five years; on land or sea, sick or well, I have remembered them before God by name . . . I shall continue to pray for them daily, by name, until they are saved, or die."

After thirty-five years of prayer, the fourth man was saved. Muller prayed for almost sixty-four years for the last friend. He wrote near the end of his life, "The great point is never to give up until the answer comes. I have been praying for sixty-three years and eight months for one man's conversion. He is not saved yet, but he will be. How can it be otherwise . . . I am praying."[2]

> There is nothing that so touches the heart of God as the certain faith of a trusting friend.

Finally, Muller died. This friend, for whom he persevered in prayer for sixty-four years, came to his funeral. And that day, when Muller's casket was lowered into the grave, there, near the open grave, this friend gave his heart to Jesus Christ.

Certainty: supreme confidence that the answer is coming from God. This isn't some manufactured faith; this isn't a trumped-up, psyched-up, pumped-up bravado. Certainty is a quiet, sure confidence that God is going to answer. This faith is developed in deep relationship with God; it isn't a hollow rally cry attempting to convince oneself of faith and make God act on my or your behalf.

There is nothing that so touches the heart of God as the certain faith of a trusting friend. George Muller made a com-

---

2 Bounds, E.M. *Power Through Prayer*, Grand Rapids, MI: Baker, 1972, p. 124-125

mitment to take care of orphans without ever asking for financial support because he wanted to prove that God still answers prayer. He wrote, "The first and primary purpose of the work was (and still is) that God might be magnified by the fact, that the orphans under my care are provided with all they need, only by prayer and faith."[3]

Muller took care of ten thousand orphans in his lifetime, and he never asked for a penny from anyone. He trusted God to intervene, and God did, but not without deep faith, persistent prayer, miraculous intervention, great sacrifice, and severe testing.

One day things looked bleak for the children in George Muller's orphanage at Ashley Downs in England. It was time for breakfast, and there was no food. A small girl whose father was a close friend of Muller was visiting in the home; she knew there was no food. Muller took her hand and said, "Come and see what our Father will do."

In the dining room, long tables were set with empty plates and empty mugs. Not only was there no food in the kitchen, there was no money in the home's account. Muller began praying: "Dear Father, we thank Thee for what Thou are going to give us to eat." Immediately, they heard a knock at the door. When they opened it, there stood the local baker. "Mr. Muller," he said, "I couldn't sleep last night. Somehow I felt you had no bread for breakfast, so I got up at 2 o'clock and baked fresh bread. Here it is."

Muller thanked him and gave praise to God. Soon, a second knock was heard. It was the milkman. His cart had broken down in front of the orphanage. He said he would like to give the children the milk so he could empty the cart and repair it.[4]

---

3 Muller, George. *Answers to Prayer*, Chicago, IL: Moody Press, 1984, p.11
4 Garton, Nancy. *George Muller and his Orphans*, Bath: Chivers, 1993, p.69

The children had breakfast that morning because George Muller lived in the realm of certain faith. The Father is irresistibly attracted to the certain faith of His children.

E.M. Bounds, in his book *Purpose in Prayer,* recalls this story about Muller, relayed from a Major D.W. Whittle. Whittle:

> I met Mr. Muller in the express, the morning of our sailing from Quebec to Liverpool. About half-an-hour before the tender was to take the passengers to the ship, he asked of the agent if a deck chair had arrived for him from New York. He was answered, 'No,' and told that it could not possibly come in time for the steamer. I had with me a chair I had just purchased, and told Mr. Muller of the place nearby, and suggested, as but a few moments remained, that he had better buy one at once. His reply was, 'No, my brother. Our Heavenly Father will send the chair from New York. It is one used by Mrs. Muller. I wrote ten days ago to a brother, who promised to see it forwarded here last week. He has not been prompt, as I would have desired, but I am sure our Heavenly Father will send the chair. Mrs. Muller is very sick on the sea, and has particularly desired to have this same chair, and not finding it here yesterday, we have made special prayer that our Heavenly Father would be pleased to provide it for us, and we will trust Him to do so.' As this dear man of God went peacefully on board, running the risk of Mrs. Muller making the trip without a chair, when, for a couple of dollars, she could have been provided for, I confess I feared Mr. Muller was carrying his faith principles too far and not acting wisely. I was kept at the express office ten minutes after Mr. Muller left. Just as I started to hurry to the wharf, a team drove up the street, and on top of a load just arrived from New York was Mr. Muller's chair. It was sent at once to the tender and placed in my hands to take to Mr. Muller, just as the boat was leaving the dock (the Lord having a lesson for me). Mr. Muller took it with the happy, pleased expression of a child who has just received a kindness deeply appreciated, and

reverently removing his hat and folding his hands over it, he thanked the Heavenly Father for sending the chair.[5]

When you develop certain faith, you believe God for the big stuff, and you don't sweat the small stuff. Muller lived in certainty almost all the time.

The following incident from the life of George Muller is related by a Mr. Inglis, who heard the story from the captain of the ship with whom Muller prayed.

> When you develop certain faith, you believe God for the big stuff, and you don't sweat the small stuff.

When I first came to America, thirty-one years ago[,] I crossed the Atlantic with the captain of a steamer who was one of the most devoted men I ever knew, and when we were off the banks of Newfoundland he said to me: Mr. Inglis, the last time I crossed here, five weeks ago, one of the most extraordinary things happened which, has completely revolutionized the whole of my Christian life. Up to that time I was one of your ordinary Christians. We had a man of God on board, George Muller, of Bristol. I had been on that bridge for twenty-two hours and never left it. I was startled by someone tapping me on the shoulder. It was George Muller: "Captain," he said, "I have come to tell you that I must be in Quebec on Saturday afternoon." This was Wednesday. "It is impossible," I said. "Very well, if your ship can't take me, God will find some other means of locomotion to take me. I have never broken an engagement in fifty-seven years." "I would willingly help you. How can I? I am helpless." "Let us go down to the chart room and pray." I looked at that man of God, and I thought

5 Bounds, E.M. *The Works of E.M. Bounds*, Zeeland, MI: Reformed Church Publications, 2009, p.156

to myself: what lunatic asylum could that man have come from? I never heard of such a thing. "Mr. Muller," I said, "do you know how dense the fog is?" "No," he replied, "my eye is not on the density of the fog, but on the living God who controls every circumstance of my life." He got down on his knees and prayed one of the most simple prayers. I muttered to myself: "That would suit a children's class where the children were not more than eight or nine years old." The burden of his prayer was something like this: "O Lord, if it is consistent with Thy will, please remove this fog in five minutes. You know the engagement you made for me in Quebec Saturday. I believe it is your will." When he finished[,] I was going to pray, but he put his hand on my shoulder and told me not to pray. "First, you do not believe He will; and second[,] I believe He has. And there is no need whatever for you to pray about it." I looked at him, and George Muller said, "Captain. I have known my Lord for fifty-seven years, and there has never been a single day that I have failed to gain an audience with the King. Get up, captain, and open the door, and you will find the fog is gone." I got up, and the fog was gone! You tell that to some people of a scientific turn of mind, and they will say, "That is not according to natural laws." No, it is according to spiritual laws. The God with whom we have to do is omnipotent. Hold on to God's omnipotence. Ask believingly. On Saturday afternoon, I may add, George Müller was there on time.[6]

George Muller developed certainty in faith; he lived his life to demonstrate the faithfulness of God in answer to prayer. And it is a stunning testimony to ponder. Muller wrote the following paragraph in his journal during a particularly difficult and trying time, when finances were always a challenge. Please, read it carefully, read it slowly, read it multiple times. It

---

6   Brooks, Phillips. "A Most Remarkable Incident." *Herald of Gospel Liberty*, Volume 102, Issues 27-52, August 1910, p. 1060

is a gripping testimony of faith.

> Though now (July 1845) for about seven years our funds have been so exhausted, that it has been a *rare* case that there have been means in hand to meet the necessities of more than 100 persons for *three days* together; yet I have been only once tried in spirit, and that was on September 18, 1838, when, for the first time the Lord seemed not to regard our prayer. But when He did send help at that time, and I saw that it was only for the trial of our faith, and not because He has forsaken the work, that we were brought so low, my soul was so strengthened and encouraged, that I have not only not been allowed to distrust the Lord, but *I have not been even cast down when in the deepest poverty* since that time.[7] (emphasis is Muller's)

Muller went through seven years of steep financial trial, never having more than three days' worth of supplies for more than one hundred orphans, and he had one day where his faith wobbled. He was never discouraged again after that one day.

I have read and reread this book because my faith has struggled in dark times. There were times discouragement felt oppressive, and I had to battle every day to get a grip on faith. The first time I read this paragraph was in a particularly dark time, and I wept as I read the words. I hit my knees and confessed my wobbly faith, and I looked to cooperate with God to move my weak and wavering faith from hope to expectation to certainty, like George Muller's.

Oh, to live our lives in such a way that we would get to Heaven and find that Jesus was

Oh, to live our lives in such a way that we would get to Heaven and find that Jesus was amazed by our great faith.

---

7 Muller, George. *Answers to Prayer*, Chicago, IL: Moody Press, 1984, p.38

amazed by our great faith. It would be a noble goal to live such a life for the honor of Jesus. Jesus has the scars to prove that He is fully worthy of our complete trust.

The Gift of Faith

Some say, "Well, it was easy for Muller because he had the gift of faith." But Muller actually wrote against that line of thinking in his book Answers to Prayer; he knew people would use that as an excuse not to develop deep faith, so he addressed it.

> Think not, dear reader, that I have the gift of faith, that is, the gift of which we read in 1 Cor. 12:9, and which is mentioned along with 'the gifts of healing,' 'the working of miracles,' 'prophecy,' and that on that account I am able to trust in the Lord. It is true that the faith, which I am enabled to exercise, is altogether God's own gift; it is true that He alone supports it, and that He alone can increase it; it is true that, moment by moment, I depend upon Him for it, and that, if I were only one moment left to myself, my faith would utterly fail; but it is not true that my faith is the gift of faith which is spoken of in 1 Cor. 12:9" (pp. 29, 30).

Muller says it is the same active faith that he had to exercise in other areas in his relationship with God. "I have never been permitted to doubt during the last sixty-nine years that my sins are forgiven, that I am a child of God, that I am beloved of God, and that I shall be finally saved; because I am enabled, by the grace of God, to exercise faith upon the word of God, and believe what God says in those passages which settle these matters" (*Answers to Prayer*, p. 30).

If we can demonstrate certain faith in one area of our lives—like believing God for our forgiveness—it is possible to develop certain faith in other areas of our lives. This is what Muller realized and lived into. But for that to happen, we must stop making excuses and justifications for our weak faith. We must admit it and determine to develop faith that is certain. We must continually look to God to strengthen our faith and not accept weak and faltering faith as a plight for which we have no control. We must take responsibility for our faith and its ongoing development by the grace of God. No complacent, passive, spiritual seeker will develop certain faith. When faith is not developed intentionally but is assumed passively, it is not developed at all.

When faith is not developed intentionally but is assumed passively, it is not developed at all.

The gift of faith is a revelatory gift. It is listed in 1 Corinthians 12 with other revelatory gifts like prophecy, a word of wisdom, a word of knowledge, and discernment. These gifts are "manifestation" gifts (1 Corinthians 12:7). Every time one of these gifts occurs, there is a manifestation of the presence of God—there is a revelation through this supernatural gift that makes God known in the moment.

The gift of faith is the ability to believe that something is going to happen because there is a supernatural revelation that brings unusual confidence to believe. When my uncle had his heart attack, God gave me a word that my uncle would not die, and with that word came the supernatural faith to believe God for his healing; that was a gift of faith for that specific occasion.

However, the certainty that I experienced in that moment for my uncle did not carry over into certainty when praying for all sick people at all times thereafter. Yet there have been other times that I have prayed for something and known deep down in my spirit that this thing would happen—that was a gift of faith. It occurs in the moment, for a specific situation, and it is revelatory gift of the Spirit. There is an assurance given by the Spirit to believe for this specific circumstance to change.

What Muller had was not a gift of faith that he exercised over and over for each day of his life for each provision for the orphans under his care. Rather, Muller developed certainty in faith through a deep and trusting relationship with a good and reliable Father. He engaged in a process of developing his faith that allowed him to grow to a place of such active trust in God that he lived with absolute confidence in God's answers to his prayer.

This active trust in God is developed in deep, intimate connection with Him. Muller wasn't praying selfish prayers for his own benefit; he was praying according to Jesus' will, but he prayed with certain faith. And when a person develops their faith so that they operate in this level of confidence and active trust, it releases the resources of Heaven to manifest the works of the Kingdom in their midst. This kind of faith can be developed, but not without time, intimacy, and a willingness to engage in the battle within.

My Own Journey of Faith

In the beginning of 2005 I called my friend Martin Sanders because I wanted to create a weekend where we could teach on the Holy Spirit and then have lab time where people could experience the workings of the Spirit. This vision arose out of my desire to see renewal and to see people operate in the power and gifts of the Spirit—just as believers did in the book of Acts. I knew a lot of people had a biblical theology of the Holy Spirit, but they hadn't integrated that belief system into their daily existence. I wanted to create an atmosphere where people could integrate their faith into their daily living.

I called Martin and explained the vision I had for this

Holy Spirit weekend. "I want to teach on prophecy," I said, "and then create a space where people can actually take time to hear from God and test it. I want to teach on healing and then have them pray for each other and see the Spirit heal and bring forth testimonies of healing from our midst. I want to teach on the filling of the Spirit and then pray for people and see the Spirit come in power."

He loved the idea, and we started doing Holy Spirit weekends. One of my primary motivations for having these weekends was wanting to see people filled with the Holy Spirit. I have an entire chapter on this in my book *River Dwellers*, but suffice it to say for now, the church in Acts was forever and dramatically changed by the Spirit's outpouring.

We need to be baptized with, or filled with, the Spirit and then we need to live in the continual fullness of the Spirit. It was my encounter of being filled with the Spirit that changed my life. I am convinced that revival is a Spirit-filled community of believers. So often we have a small number of people who are walking in the current fullness of the Spirit, but for revival to occur, we need a community of people who experience the fullness of the Spirit and then walk in the fullness of the Spirit. So, I wanted to teach on the filling of the Spirit and then create a lab time where we laid hands on people and prayed for the Holy Spirit to come.

In the beginning, when I taught on the baptism of the Spirit and laid hands on people, not much happened. At best, I hoped *something* would happen. Occasionally, we would see a person filled with the Spirit; we might see one or two people filled with the Spirit in a Holy Spirit weekend. The manifest presence of God would come, and someone would be drenched with the love of God. But it was only occasionally. My faith could not sustain the answer that I sought. It had to be developed from hope, to expectation, to certainty.

We kept doing Holy Spirit weekends, and in every weekend

that I participated in I made sure we included a talk on the baptism or filling of the Spirit. It has now been more than a dozen years, and I have taught in dozens of Holy Spirit weekends at South Shore Community Church, where I pastor, and around the world. There has been a dramatic shift through the years.

I started seeing the shift a few years back after coming out of one of my darkest seasons in life and ministry. Now when we do a Holy Spirit weekend in a place where people have been properly prepared, and we lay hands on people, we will see dozens of people filled with the Spirit. The manifest presence of God will come, and some will be drenched with God's love, others will be overwhelmed by God's presence and fall to the ground like John the Apostle did (Revelation 1:17), and others will be filled to overflowing with joy and the presence of God. God comes in power.

I no longer *hope* God will show up at these times. I don't even *expect* God will show up at these times; I am *certain* God will show up, and with power. I am not certain that every person will have the same encounter, or every person I pray for will necessarily be drenched with his love or fall over in his presence. But I am certain that the dozens of people in the crowd will be filled every single time we teach on the filling of the Spirit and pray for people to be filled. If I pray for fifty people who are prepared and ready, the majority of them will encounter God.

The major difference between what happens today and what happened at the beginning is faith. God has taken me on a journey to develop my faith so my faith can sustain the answer to the prayer I prayed.

How do you develop faith that releases the works of the Kingdom? How do you develop faith that allows the presence and power of God to flow? Jesus said, "Very truly I tell you, all who have faith in me will do the works I have been doing, and

54

they will do even greater things than these." The key is faith. We all have nothing; we come with empty hands.

But some, like Muller, come with their empty hands and a supreme confidence in the One whose hands are full of all we need. They look to Him with an unshakable faith that releases the resources of Heaven. How do we develop a faith like that? That's what we will explore for the rest of the book.

Reflection Questions

1. Think about a time when you had certain faith for something: the forgiveness of sins, the healing of a loved one, financial provision. Why was your faith certain at that time? What prepared you to have certain faith?

2. In what areas is your faith the strongest?

3. Are there any areas of your life in which you are wrestling with unbelief? Not just doubt, but unbelief? Take time to allow the Holy Spirit to show you any areas of unbelief and repent.

4. Where does your faith need development? In what areas are you struggling to believe?

Three:
Intimacy with God

"Never be afraid to trust an unknown future to a known God."
—Corrie ten Boom

"Faith is not belief without proof,
but trust without reservation."

—Elton Trueblood

"If the Lord fails me at this time, it will be the first time."

—George Muller

There are some people in my life, like my wife and some of my dear friends, with whom I can share anything. I don't have any secrets with these people; they know all there is to know about me. Why? The key is trust. I trust them because they are people of character and integrity, compassion, and honor. I have opened up to them, and they have proven trustworthy with my heart. They have seen my best and worst and accepted me for who I am.

Trust is the foundation of healthy, deep, intimate relation-

> If you are going to develop faith, you must draw near to God and discover that He can be fully trusted.

ships. This is the same way our relationship with God operates. If you are going to develop faith, you must draw near to God and discover that He can be fully trusted. Developing intimacy with God takes time and effort—just like developing intimacy with a spouse.

Jen and I had to spend time together, open our hearts together, learn how to honor one another, work through conflict together, forgive one another, process pain together, and go through a host of other soul-wrenching, relationship-building activities.

Trust was developed in the trenches, over time, with much commitment and effort, and it is no different with God. In this chapter we will explore some key principles to developing deep, intimate trust with God.

Principles for Developing Deep Trust

Principle 1: Wrestle with Hard Things

To develop closeness with God that leads to deep trust, you must wrestle with hard things honestly and honorably. No one escapes this life without suffering, and unprocessed suffering leads to distrust. You must process your suffering and hardship openly and honestly in order to keep your heart soft and accessible to God.

> To develop closeness with God that leads to deep trust, you must wrestle with hard things honestly and honorably.

I grew up in the church, so in the beginning I went to church because my parents went. If you grow up in a non-Christian home and you come to faith, your journey will often involve a conversion experience in which you encounter God's love and forgiveness. This deposits trust in your soul bank account.

I trusted Christ when I was about seven years old. Jesus was just part of my upbringing, and I accepted many of the truths of Christianity because my parents and my church taught them to me. But when I was about sixteen, I started reading the Bible on my own. It was my first venture at forging my own relationship with God, and I started wrestling with God honestly, right at the beginning of our relationship.

A pastor challenged our church to read the Bible in a year, and I took up the challenge. The first time I read through the Bible, there were a lot of things I didn't understand, and there were some things that caused me to struggle with my faith, to wrestle with the goodness of God. This was an important part of my journey because I was developing my own faith, and I had to sort through these things before I could trust God. If I ignored the questions that emerged within me when I read the Bible, I would have struggled with underlying distrust. I had to question; I had to wrestle. I had to decide if I could trust God with my life.

I remember the first time I read the book of Exodus and got to the part where God hardened Pharaoh's heart. I could not understand this. It didn't make sense. Why would God do that? Why wouldn't God draw this man to Himself? Why wouldn't He woo him? How could God make it so the man's heart was hard and unresponsive? Why would He intentionally turn anyone away from Himself? It made me angry. I had to struggle with what God is like, and why God does what He does; I had to wrestle with God's goodness and whether I trusted Him.

There were many other portions of Scripture that caused me to ask the same questions and wrestle deeply with what I had been taught. I had been taught that God was good, but I read some things that seemed to contradict that assertion, and I didn't have enough personal history and experience with God to simply accept what I had been taught. But I didn't stop reading just because I struggled to understand and questioned God's actions and goodness. I kept reading, kept exploring, kept wrestling. I talked to God about the things I didn't understand.

> Deep faith seldom comes easily; it is a faith that is tried and tested. Just like intimacy in human relationships, a deep and active trust in God comes through many valleys.

After I finished reading through the Bible the first time, when I was sixteen, I turned back to the beginning and read through it again. And again. And again. I felt a bit like Peter and the disciples in John 6 when the crowds left Jesus because of his teaching. He turned to the disciples and said, "Are you going to leave too?" And Peter said, "Where would we go? You have the words of life." I felt like that. There was life here; Jesus was undeniably appealing. But some of what I read was so hard to understand, and I had to wrestle with it openly and honestly with God.

Deep faith seldom comes easily; it is a faith that is tried and tested. Just like intimacy in human relationships, a deep and active trust in God comes through many valleys. The many valleys Jen and I have shared together caused us to struggle and sort through things, but when we came out the other side, we trusted each other more deeply and loved each other more. The key to our deepest levels of intimacy was conflict handled well.

I have gone through dark valleys with God where I prayed

for deliverance from some issue, but deliverance did not come. I struggled with why God didn't answer the way I wanted. I struggled with feeling disappointed. But again and again in these dark places, I discovered God was with me. I learned things about God in the struggle that I could not have learned in a quick and easy solution. And I grew in the struggle in ways that I could not have grown with a quick and easy answer to prayer. One of our problems is that we tend to overvalue the short term and undervalue the long view. We tend to overvalue comfort and ease and undervalue growth and development. If God answered some of my prayers in the short run, my character may not have been developed sufficiently, and it may have derailed my long term spiritual development and journey. The God of the cross redeems every valley in the life of the willing follower.

It was often during these difficult times that I grew the most and experienced God's presence the strongest, heard God's voice the clearest, and experienced God's transforming work the deepest. But I had to wrestle honestly and honorably. I had to process my emotions, and I had to surrender to the King. I could not surrender without the struggle. Every surrender is a death to self. I have been with people when they die; I have seen people in the throes of death, right before people "give up the ghost." It is a struggle, but when a person dies and gives up their spirit, the body settles into rest. This is true of surrender; I have to struggle as I die to self, but when I surrender, die to self, and "give up the ghost," peace comes. Too often people resort to trite religious clichés to get them through deep valleys. But if the cliché is not a deeply held, internalized truth, then it will only breed shallow faith. It is better to sincerely wrestle with the deep questions of the heart, and truly surrender, than it is to quote an easy Sunday School answer and bury unprocessed emotion that fuels our distrust.

In the dark times, I discovered that God doesn't always

work the way I want, but I can trust Him. God is not always on my timetable, but He is always on time. Waiting, displaying patience, and surrendering to God's plan and timing is hard, but it is fundamentally important to developing deep trust.

You have to develop your own history with God, your own experiences with God, and your own relationship with God to develop trust. And like other relationships on the human level, deep trust takes time to develop. At the time of this writing (2016), I've been married for 26 years. There are times the thought processes and actions of my wife have been baffling to me. If she were writing, she would probably say that there are times my thoughts and behaviors make her scratch her head too. But I have developed deep trust with Jen. Why? She is a person of character; she is one of the most honest people I know, and that is irresistibly attractive to me. The things that matter to God matter to Jen, and I respect her. I developed a deep trust with her over time, and I had to do the same in my relationship with God.

Don't shrink back from wrestling with the questions that undermine your faith. But keep coming to God. I encourage you to wrestle honorably because trust is never built in atmospheres of dishonor. I let all of my raw emotion out; I don't filter any of my hurt, disappointment, anger, fear, or any other negative emotion that I am experiencing. But I treat God with honor, respect, dignity, and reverence as I process. Dishonoring God will quench the Spirit and not help me develop deep trust. As you wrestle and process honestly and honorably, use all the human resources available to you. Tap into wise and compassionate people with great understanding of the things of God, and wrestle it through. Read the books of great saints who have struggled through dark times; this will help you process and develop deep faith.

Principle 2: The Jesus Factor

> To develop intimacy with God that leads to deep trust, you must read all of the Scriptures in light of the revelation of Jesus.

To develop intimacy with God that leads to deep trust, you must read all of the Scriptures in light of the revelation of Jesus.

As I started to develop my own trust relationship with God, I discovered that the person of the Trinity I connected with most was Jesus. I couldn't get enough of the gospels, and I couldn't get enough of Jesus. He was the most compelling person I had ever met, studied, and encountered. I loved Him. Jesus was my bridge to understanding God, and to holding to trust in my most incomprehensible moments.

Hebrews 1:1-3 says, "In the past God spoke to our ancestors through the prophets at many times and in various ways, but in these last days he has spoken to us by his Son, whom he appointed heir of all things, and through whom also he made the universe. The Son is the radiance of God's glory and the exact representation of his being."

Jesus perfectly *re-presents* and represents the Father to us. If you want to know what the Father is like, look to Jesus— He is the one the Father sent to show us what He Himself is like. This helped me immeasurably, because while I struggled with parts of the Old Testament to understand the heart of God, when I looked to Jesus and I held closely to this verse in Hebrews, I knew that the Father was just like Jesus, even if I couldn't understand or couldn't see clearly yet. Holding on to what God said about Himself, and how God represented Himself through Jesus, was fundamental to the development of my deep faith. The Father knew that in this darkened world that has been tainted and twisted by evil, we will struggle to trust that He is good, so He sent us Jesus so we can know what He is truly like. The Father sent Jesus so that even when we can't fully comprehend, we can still trust.

I struggled with the goodness of God at times because of the evil in the world. When I started reading Scripture, I struggled with parts of the Old Testament. I wrestled with the goodness of God because I read stories of judgment, like when He called the Israelites to wipe out surrounding tribes of people. I felt God was harsh, and I floundered in my trust. But if Jesus was the exact representation of the Father, then through the cross I found the true heart of God. I kept coming back to the cross so I could develop trust in the tenderness of God that was often hard to see.

An important phrase began emerging for me: I cannot always understand why things happen, but I know I can trust God because of the cross. On the cross, God proved his love for me. I had to continually reinterpret the events of life and history through the lens of the cross. The cross is God's perpetual reminder to us that He cares.

I know many people struggle, because of the pain and suffering on our planet, to believe that God is good. I know many people read certain sections of Scripture and are blinded to the goodness of God. There are many things in this world that we will not understand completely until we get to Heaven, but even so, we can trust God is good in light of the cross. I cannot understand all of Scripture completely this side of Heaven. But in Jesus, I can be certain of the love of God for me and the goodness of God in all things. When I look to Jesus, I can be sure that God is for me and not against me. The incarnation of Jesus reminds us that God did not abandon us in the harshness of our broken, fallen world. He became one of us. He suffered as we suffer. In the cross, I see the eternal love of a Father who was determined to find a way to be reconciled to his children. I see a Father who dealt with the real problems created by sin. I see a Father who refused to quit on a rebellious creation.

God did not sit on his throne in Heaven aloof to human sin, pain, and suffering. He entered *into* our suffering; He suffered with us, and He suffered for us. On the cross, Jesus took up our sin, our shame, our suffering, our sickness, and our death. He took up all the pain and suffering created by evil and sin, and He reminded us once and for all that God cares, God redeems. The bloodstains of Jesus are the prevailing proof that God cares for us. He is not passive in his love for us, no matter how life's circumstances—tainted by the brokenness of our world—may seem to indicate that He is indifferent and passive. The cross shouts to us that He is an active, passionate lover who is ever caring, ever engaging. In Jesus' life, I see the heart of the Father as He opens the eyes of the blind, touches the leper, delivers the demonized, raises the dead, and feeds the hungry. Reading all of Scripture, and looking across all the events in life, in light of Jesus' coming and dying and rising again helped me catch a true glimpse of God. And it also enabled me to develop a deeper trust in a good Father.

Principle 3: Spending Time Alone with God

To develop intimacy with God that leads to deep trust, you must spend time alone with God.

I made a critically important decision when I was in my early twenties: I decided that I would make spending time with God the number one priority of my life. The first commandment is to love God with all our heart, soul, mind, and strength, because God is the most important person. If God is the most im-

> To develop intimacy with God that leads to deep trust, you must spend time alone with God.

portant person, worthy of our total heart's affections, then I had to make spending time with God my number one priority.

I decided spending time with God would hit my calendar first; it would be a nonnegotiable in my life. I am sure that I could not have worked my way through the rough spots, and could not have developed a deeper faith, if it were not for this landmark decision in my life. It was like my covenant commitment to Jen to stay married "till death do us part." When Jen and I struggled with our deepest conflicts, this covenant we made with one another made us committed to find a way through the valley. I remember one season in our life when we talked every night and felt like we weren't making any progress. But we would end every conflicted conversation with this phrase: "Divorce is not an option. We will find our way through with the help of God." And we did. But we found resolutions because we were committed to the relationship; we committed to keep talking, keep listening, keep trying, until we finally made it through. My commitment to spend time alone with God saw me through every valley, every thicket, and every spiritual swamp and wasteland.

I have pastored people for nearly thirty years, and one of the hardest parts of doing so is watching people walk away from their faith. Too often, people walk away because life gets hard, they get hurt, they take offense at God, they don't process their hurts and disappointments, and they give up. If only they would persist, if only they would keep talking, keep processing, keep seeking, eventually they would find their way through. I often wonder how many people quit just before they are about to break through. Keep spending time with God; you can't break through without it.

In the beginning, I spent time alone with God by practicing the only two spiritual disciplines I had been taught: I read my Bible and prayed. Most of my prayers consisted of intercession and petition, though I did a fair bit of arguing with

God, questioning God, and pleading with God as I wrestled with things I did not understand. This was part of seeking, part of developing intimacy, part of coming to deep faith.

One of the reasons I loved the Psalms, and still do, is because the psalmists are so brutally honest with God. They are reverent and honoring but fearlessly frank with God about their emotions, struggles, confusion, hurts, and dismay over God's apparent inactivity at times in their lives. And yet God isn't put off by it at all—He actually seems to welcome it and be drawn to it. Honest seekers after God wrestle deeply with the dark places of their soul in order to develop deep faith. And this was a big part of my faith journey, early on, and all along the way.

Through the years I found other spiritual activities that allowed me to connect deeply with God, and I practiced new spiritual disciplines like personal private worship, listening prayer, meditation on Scripture, silence and solitude, and many others. Here is the main point: I never stopped spending time with God. I have changed my approach to seeking God over the years; I have changed the spiritual practices I engage in and how frequently I engage in them. I have spent considerable time at a local monastery, seeking God through fasting and sacrificial pursuit of God. But the one thing I never did was go back on my primary commitment—spending time with God would be my number one priority. That commitment saw me through every dark valley. Many people make the mistake of giving up on their time with God when they get busy or disappointed. Faith isn't developed in disengagement; faith is developed in seeking after God.

Principle 4: Surrender

To develop intimacy with God that leads to deep trust, you must surrender. You can only respond to God in three ways:

> To develop intimacy with God that leads to deep trust, you must surrender.

you can rebel, resign, or surrender.

When life gets hard, many people opt for rebellion. They get angry at God, they shake their fist at God, and they act in rebellion, abandoning God's way and opting for their own way.

Some people resign. Resignation occurs when we feel like there is nothing we can do, life is hard, God isn't responding, and we are powerless to do anything about it. We can't overcome, we can't make God do what we want, so we just resign. We give up the struggle, the wrestling, the dialogue, and the working out of trust. This leads to a hopelessness. People who resign often don't walk away from God or the church, but they have no passion, no energy, and very little trust.

Both rebellion and resignation are rooted in distrust. Only surrender is rooted in trust. When we surrender, we trust the character and goodness of God so much that in spite of the circumstances that surround us, we yield ourselves to God and go his way. We choose to actively trust God, sort out our disarray of emotions, and bow our stiff necks to God. We don't demand that God plays by our rules.

In the early part of my journey I struggled with faith. I argued and wrestled with the things I didn't understand, and, like the psalmists, I brought my struggles honestly to God. I held on to Jesus' representation of the Father, and I surrendered over and over to the God I could trust as I looked to the cross. I was making progress in faith, but it was slow. I came to realize there are some things I will never understand, some things that, as the Bible says, are "too wonderful for me"— they are beyond my comprehension. But I had enough reasons to trust, and I surrendered to the goodness of the God of the cross.

When I find myself tempted to rebel or resign, I know I must fortify my trust and choose to surrender. I choose to look to the cross. The only proper response to the God of the cross is the way of the cross; we must pick up our cross and follow Him. I remind myself of the ultimate proof of God's tender concern and trustworthy heart: the cross. I review my personal history with God. I remember the other times in my life in which I surrendered and God came through. I remember the dark valleys, where God has met me and redeemed my suffering. The more I remember my personal history, the more I realize I can trust Him in the present. I remind myself that God redeems all things, as Paul said in Romans 8. He can take even the evil things of this world and redeem them for good because He is so good. And I remind myself that I am just passing through this world, and my true citizenship is in Heaven, where God will rule in all his goodness and evil will be vanquished forever.

I try to lift my eyes off of my temporary circumstances and remind myself of this eternal perspective. Often we are praying for something to come about. It may even be a promise from God. But we may be at the beginning of the promise. Hebrews 11 records a long list of faith heroes who hold on to promises from God and see God deliver. But, then there were others – who are tortured, murdered, abused, persecuted, and forgotten (Hebrews 11:32-40). The author says, "These were all commended for their faith, yet none of them received what had been promised, since God had planned something better for us so that only together with us would they be made perfect" (39-40).

God had given them a promise; they had trusted God for the promise and held on to the promise, but they did not receive the promise. They thought the promise was for them, and held on to it faithfully expecting it to be fulfilled in their lifetime, but they were a link in the chain of an eternal family.

Only together with us was their promise fulfilled – they had received a promise that they fought for, and we received it.

There are other promises that we must fight for in our generation that only the next generation will see fulfilled. We must see ourselves in this eternal family, part of this eternal chain, and we must be willing to take this eternal perspective and surrender to God wherever we find ourselves in the process. Sometimes we are at the beginning of the chain – and we will not see the promise. Sometimes we are at the end of the chain, and we get to see the promise fulfilled that someone else fought for. We will never come to trusting surrender without understanding the eternal perspective of God.

The more I focus on these noble things, the more my heart trusts and is prepared to surrender. Prepare your heart and surrender. The more you surrender, the deeper your trust will go.

Principle 5: Encounters with God

To develop intimacy with God that leads to deep trust, you must encounter God. It is not enough to know about God; you must know God personally, and this requires revelation from the Holy Spirit.

> To develop intimacy with God that leads to deep trust, you must encounter God.

I write books, and I tell a lot of personal stories in those books. When I travel to speak, it is not uncommon for someone to approach me and say, "I feel like I know you because I've read your books." They do know *about* me, but they don't know me. They have read about me, they may know people who know me, but they have no personal history with me or relational experience with me. This is, sadly, also all too true of too many people as they relate to God—they have read about Him in a book, and they know someone who knows Him. But this won't build deep trust. We need a personal relationship with God that yields something more than cognitive knowledge; we need personal experience in order to develop deep trust.

The game changer for me in the early days of my relationship with God was a personal encounter with God. I was in my freshman year in college when I had this first encounter. I had been pursuing God, reading Scripture, wrestling with the deep questions that undermined my faith, and asking God to show Himself to me—and He finally did.

I was driving home after a breakup. I pulled off to the side of the road and called out to God, and He met me. The love of God was poured out in my heart like Paul speaks of in Romans 5. I tell this full story in *River Dwellers*, and you can read it there. It was a supernatural filling of the Spirit; I was drenched with his loving presence.

The important part of the story for this context is that it shifted the way I trusted God. Personal experience and supernatural revelation made all the difference. When the Spirit reveals the love of God to you, you cannot help but see the world through different lenses; you cannot help but read the Scriptures with new perspective. My wife told me that when she first got her glasses as a young girl, she remembered driving home and seeing the leaves on the trees. Before she had glasses the trees were just a blur of green; with those glasses, she could see the distinction of the individual leaves.

Encounters with God help us make sense of the details of our life in light of the goodness of God. When the love of God is made known in your heart, you cannot help but develop trust at deeper levels. When the love of God becomes part of your own personal testimony, things you once questioned are now answered—not because you have actual answers, but because you trust the One who loves you so deeply. Overwhelmed by love and the knowing of God, these other things become nonissues. When the love of God moves from a concept that you believe to a reality that you experience, you are developing your own history with God, and you know that God is good and God is trustworthy.

> When the love of God moves from a concept that you believe to a reality that you experience, you are developing your own history with God, and you know that God is good and God is trustworthy.

After my encounter with God, I read the Bible and saw things that I had never seen before. I noticed, for example, in the passage in Exodus, that God didn't harden Pharaoh's heart until after Pharaoh had hardened his own heart. I never noticed that when my relationship with God was undermined by distrust. Trust opens your heart to fresh revelation; distrust fuels misunderstanding of the heart of God.

After my personal encounter with God's deep love, I no longer read the Scriptures with the suspicious eyes of a distrusting observer. Now I viewed the Scriptures as looking to discover the truth about the God I loved, because He first loved me. Only then did I notice that Pharaoh chose first to harden his heart, and this after God had given him opportunities to repent, which Pharaoh refused. Before that encounter I could only see the harshness of God; after that encounter I could see the goodness and mercy of God on every page. Your personal history with God affects the way you see the world, read the Bible, and interpret the experiences of life.

I want to offer one caution for pursuing God. You need to pursue God's face with a theology of power. Don't seek power; seek God for *Himself*, but hold on to a theological understanding of God's supernatural capacity to intervene in this world with miraculous power while you seek his face. Too often we seek God not to know God but to have more from God. We want to feel better; we want an answer to prayer; we want a miracle, a healing, a provision. *Seek Him for Himself.* Intimacy builds trust; we must get to know Him.

Jesus promised that all who believed would do the works He had been doing, but sometimes we pursue God because we want to see God move in power. One of my favorite verses in Scripture is John 15:5: "I am the vine; you are the branches. If you remain in me and I in you, you will bear much fruit; apart from me you can do nothing." This verse had such an impact in my life that I was often motivated to seek God because I knew I needed his anointing. I knew I could do nothing of eternal significance and Kingdom impact without the presence and power of Jesus in my life. But I found myself seeking God's hands, not his face. I was seeking God for what He could do, not for intimacy with Him.

When I approached the age of forty, my heart started longing for something more. I longed to know God, not just serve God or bear Kingdom fruit for God. I started seeking God's face, not just his hands. Pursuing God's face also changed the way I approached my time with Him. I did less asking and more worship. I spent less time talking and more time listening. I spent less time trying to accomplish things in prayer and more time being with Him.

The shift was significant. I began to seek God's face with a theology of power, and I noticed that power followed. The power was a direct result of the increase of his presence in my life. As God became my first pursuit, the things of the Kingdom that were the desire of my heart became more regularly manifest in my life and ministry. Where God is more present, his power is more evident.

It is not unlike the shift that takes place over time in the relationship between a child and a parent. In the beginning, the child comes to the parent because he or she needs something; he needs food, comfort, help, instruction, or money. But later on in life as the child grows into maturity, the child comes to the parent for relationship. The good parent is no less likely to serve the child, to give to the child, to be generous with the child; perhaps the good parent is more likely to give because the relationship is growing deeper.

So it is with our relationship with the Father. When you pursue the Father for his face with a theology of power, when you pursue Him for intimacy, then you will often see more answers to prayer that result from the increase in his presence in your life. But even when answers to prayer don't come, you discover that He is what you need most, not what He can give you.

Faith Busters

Developing a deep, trusting, intimate relationship with God is key to deepening your faith, and there are certain things that hinder or limit your faith. These faith busters ultimately hinder your intimacy with God, and that is why they impair the development of our faith. Let's look at three: sin, fear, and disappointments.

Sin

Sometimes our faith is impaired by sin. We have to walk in the light with God and others (1 John 1). We have to acknowledge and confess our sin so the blood of Christ can cleanse us and we can be restored to a right relationship with God and others.[8]

---

8 The concept of walking in the light with God and others is discussed extensively in *Soul Care: 7 Transformational Principles for a Healthy Soul*.

Sin hinders the flow of the Spirit; sin stunts our spiritual growth. Some sins are obvious, and we are well aware of them. Paul writes to the Colossians: "Put to death, therefore, whatever belongs to your earthly nature: sexual immorality, impurity, lust, evil desires and greed, which is idolatry" (3:5). These are obvious, external, behavioral sins. But Paul doesn't stop there, because he knew they had mostly dealt with these issues. He continues, "You used to walk in these ways, in the life you once lived. But now you must also rid yourselves of all such things as these: anger, rage, malice, slander, and filthy language from your lips" (v. 7). Paul shifts from some obvious things to things of the heart. They still have some manifestations in actions, but these are deeper, heart-level issues like bitter roots or envy or selfish ambition.

Often, for us to reach deeper levels of intimacy with God, we must go deeper in our purity, and we have to move beyond the outward expressions of sins of action to the sins of the heart. It is often the attitudes of the heart that keep us from deep faith. It is harder to root out the sins of the heart because no one sees them, and we are often unaware of them. For example, when I was seeking God so that I could bear fruit, I had mixed motives. There were some good motives: I wanted to bear fruit for God's glory; I wanted to see people come to Christ; I wanted to see lives changed, captives set free, the poor cared for; I wanted to see the Kingdom come. But there were also some selfish motives: I wanted to bear fruit; notice the emphasis on I. I wanted to bear fruit because it made me feel good, because I liked success, because it looked good, and because I am a type A personality, wired for productivity. God wanted relationship; I wanted fruit bearing. I pursued Him because I knew I couldn't bear fruit without Him, but He wanted me to pursue Him for Himself.

Jesus didn't command us to bear fruit; He commanded us to abide. Fruit bearing is a by-product of abiding, but we can't abide in deep intimacy if we are focused on fruit bearing as our primary motivation for being with God. I had to make the shift from doing to *being*, from seeking his hands to seeking his face.

I got to a place where I was frustrated because I wasn't seeing the fruit I wanted to see. We had planted a church in New England, which isn't known for being kind to church planters, and we saw hundreds of people come to Christ. The church grew, but still I wasn't satisfied. I wanted more.

Holy discontent is a good thing. It leads us to live for Jesus and to seek to make a difference in the world for the glory of God. We want to leave the world a better place and see more people know God and experience all his freedom, love, and joy. I wanted to see the gates of hell stormed so hell could be emptied out, and Heaven populated, so that none should perish.

But holy discontent easily slips into unholy discontent, and that is what happened to me. And this is what happens to all of us when we have not rooted out the sins of the heart. The impure motives that were underneath my desire to put fruit bearing over intimacy led me to grumble and complain. Impure motives eventually surface, and without purging, faith is stunted. I took offense at God because He wasn't showing up like I wanted. I was working hard for Him, and He wasn't holding up his end of the bargain.

> Your next level of intimacy with God is always preceded by a new level of purification. You must embrace the process.

We cannot act in faith while we are grumbling and complaining. Grumbling and complaining are rooted in distrust, not active trust. But this was the thing, in the end, that caused me to seek God. God started purifying my heart motivations and stirred within me a desire for Him. I had to repent of my offense, and my impure motives, and begin to seek his face. I longed to be with Him, not just to bear fruit. I longed to see his face, not just to seek his hands. This was a subtle sin of the heart that the Spirit needed to reveal so He could change a motivation deep within me.

Your next level of intimacy with God is always preceded by a new level of purification. You must embrace the process. Where is the Spirit seeking to purify you now? Is abiding your first priority?

Fear

We must process our fear if we are going to develop deep faith. We can either act on fear or we can act on faith, but we cannot act on both. We can act on faith while we feel afraid, but we cannot act on both—we must choose.

The people of God make more mistakes in times of fear than any other time. Fear often leads us to distrust and to act in rebellion against God. This is why the number one command in Scripture is "fear not." This command occurs more in the Bible than any other command, because God knows how spiritually paralyzing fear is. The Father knows that fear feeds distrust. George Muller said, "The beginning of anxiety is the end of faith, and the beginning of true faith is the end of anxiety."

Often your fear causes you to act in ways of unbelief, and it hinders the activity of God in your life. When you pray fear-based prayers, it only reinforces the fear in your life; God doesn't answer fear-based prayers. You must make your way out of fear and into faith.

I have never considered myself a fearful person. In my book *Soul Care*, I talk about how I came to realize that I had a root fear, and how God met me and helped me overcome.

But the older I get, the more I have become aware of the subtle role fear plays in my life and how it undermines my trust and faith in God.

Years ago, God gave me multiple promises about revival; the promises came through various means. I had a dream, which I speak about in both *Pathways to the King* and *River Dwellers*, in which a prophetess spoke to me about a coming revival and my role in the revival. At the end of the dream a sign was given to me: the sign of the coming revival was that the New Orleans Saints would win the Super Bowl. The dream was in December 2006, and the Saints won the Super Bowl in February 2010. There were other prophetic words and whispers from the Spirit that were confirmed by various means. So I started acting in faith on what the Lord had told me. I preached on revival, because the Lord told me to preach on revival until it came. I prayed for revival; I fought for revival. But while I followed through with what I believed the Lord was telling me, circumstances at the church I pastor got worse.

People got upset, angry, used Facebook to write against me, and blogged against me. People left the church and were divisive. In the beginning, I pressed on with great faith and determination because I was convinced the breakthrough was right around the corner; I processed my hurt and blessed those who cursed me and forgave those who sinned against me.

But as time went on, and circumstances didn't improve; my faith wobbled. There were times I struggled to believe the promise. I couldn't make sense of the circumstances in light of the things God told me.

This is often the way God works; there is often a lag time between the promise and its fulfillment, and that lag time can be long and hard. It is a dark valley where fears flourish and our faith is tested. God told Abraham he would have a promised child, but then there was a long gap between when the promise was given and when it was delivered. Twenty-five years went by before the child came.

When you read the story on the pages of Scripture, it doesn't feel that long, and when you see that ultimately God delivers, it sure is easy to bypass the pain of those twenty-five years. But we didn't have to live it; it is much easier to read someone else's story than to live your own. God is not always on our timetable, but He is always on time. Waiting and displaying patience is hard, but it is fundamentally important to mature trust.

David was promised that he would become king, but there was a gap between the time the promise was given and the promise delivered. It was a gap from hell—literally. A demonized king chased David and sought to take his life; David did nothing but honor Saul, and yet he was persecuted and mistreated. A life of authentic faith and deep-seated trust in a good Father is not for the faint of heart. It is filled with ups and downs, highs and lows, jagged mountain peaks and deep valleys. It is a life filled with testing, trials, and tribulation. The path to promise fulfillment is not a straight and direct route but a winding, circuitous route littered with delays, disappointments, and discouragement. It is a life fraught with fits of fear.

All of it, if we process it well, serves to purge us of our fears and false motives and prepares us to receive the promises of God. But it isn't easy. Developing faith is a hard, painful, treacherous journey. The process forms faith in us and prepares us as vessels ready to receive the promise. Muller said, "The only way to learn strong faith is to endure great trials." We all want strong faith, but are we willing to endure great trials to get there?

I had no idea what I was in for, but I said yes to God and buckled my seatbelt for the ride of a lifetime. The first few years as I preached revival and dissension stirred, there was a lot of pain and loss. We lost people, I lost friends, my reputation took a huge hit, and the finances of the church were severely impacted.

But when the Saints won the Super Bowl I was elated, and life was breathed into the promise of God. If I expected that the fulfillment of the sign would be followed with an immediate fulfillment of the promise, I was in for another disappointing surprise. That must have been how David felt when he won the great victory over Goliath and got married to the king's daughter. It surely looked like he was on a path to the throne room—signs that the promise was coming soon. But things got dramatically worse for David; those apparent signs of victory only led to his darkest valley.

As I write these words, it has been almost ten years since I received that initial promise with the sign; it has been almost seven years since the sign was fulfilled. There are areas in my life where I can see significant fulfillment, such as the impartation of the Spirit I spoke of earlier. As I travel and speak, I see more spiritual hunger than I ever have; I see more openness, even desperation, for the things of the Spirit than I ever have. But there are other areas where I can see no progress at all. I have had to battle against fears. There have been times my mind has raced with worry and concern about the present and the future. I have had to battle against discouragement; I have felt oppressed at times by the weight of discouragement along the way. My faith has wobbled, but through the struggle it has also developed. The battle has strengthened my faith because I continued to spend time with God, hold on to Jesus, process my fear and pain, remember the promises, and refuse to let go.

God always seems to give us what we need along the way to deepen our intimacy and nurture our faith, and to steady our trust in Him. But we must utilize these tools, these lifelines He throws our way. That original dream with the sign has been a great lifeline. I have often contended for the promises of God with the promises of God. Almost every day, I meditate on and pray over the promises that God has given me for revival and other things as well.

The fulfillment of the sign, the Saints winning the Super Bowl, was a great gift to me. I write about prophecy in *River Dwellers,* and I talk about the need to test prophecy. I realize that every dream isn't from God, that every whisper we hear isn't from God. They all need to be tested carefully. 1 Thessalonians 5:19-21 says: "Do not put out the Spirit's fire. Do not treat prophecies with contempt, but test them all" (TNIV). I would have been willing to dismiss the dream if it weren't for the sign. You can't make that stuff up; that sign proved to me that the dream was clearly from God. I can't tell you how many times I battled against discouragement and was ready to give up on the fight for revival, only to be steadied by the Saints' victory in the Super Bowl. I went out and bought a Saints hat, and I wear it occasionally just to remind me of the veracity and ultimate faithfulness of the promises of God.

Even before I had the dream, God threw me a lifeline. Every day in my time alone with Him, I heard these words, "Don't be afraid." And, "Fear not, for I am with you." Every time I listened, this was the first thing God would say to me. This went on for months. One day I realized that God had been saying this to me for months, and I said, "Lord, I am not afraid. Why do you keep saying this to me?" He said, "You aren't afraid, but you will be."

He was preparing me for the dark days that were ahead; He was strengthening me for the battle, nurturing my faith so that it would survive the time of testing. He is so kind. He is a good Father, and He wants to nurture our faith. He has given us lifelines that we can hold to during our darkest days. These were prepared by God to help us triumph over our fears and deepen our faith.

We must continually look over our history with God for these lifelines He has thrown us, and we must review them often and hold to them with tenacity in our darkest hours. You and I will always be tempted to forget what God has spoken to us in the light when the times of darkness come. We will be tempted to let go of the lifelines, but we must hold to these lifelines the Father throws us with a fierce tenacity to overcome the darkness. They are the tools to help us overcome our fears and strengthen our faith along the road to victory.

The greatest lifeline of all is the cross. It is in that great redemptive act of sacrificial love that we find our greatest security, our greatest comfort, and our greatest hope and help in time of need. The cross simply solidifies the reality for all eternity that we have a good Father who cares for us.

Faith is taking God at his word. It is active trust in the goodness and character of God. "Now faith is being sure of what we hope for and certain of what we do not see" (Hebrews 11:1, NIV 1984). Augustine said, "Faith is to believe what we do not see; and the reward of this faith is to see what we believe." Andrew Murray said, "What now is faith? Nothing other than the certainty that what God says is true." And Elton Trueblood: "Faith is not belief without proof, but trust without reservation." And we cannot trust God like this unless we deal with our fears and overcome them.

John wrote, "There is no fear in love. But perfect love drives out fear" (1 John 4:18). It is the perfect love of God in Christ that is the key to overcoming our fears. We must meditate on God's love in times of fear; we must renew our minds with the promises of God; we must remember the cross and recall those times when God has met us, revealed his love to us, and made his love personal. We must seek God for his face and ask Him to reveal his love to us. It is the revelation of God's love that solidifies our trust in Him. Remember all of these expressions of God's love with gratitude until fear dissipates and faith rises out of the darkness.

Disappointments

Finally, we must deal with our disappointments if we are going to develop faith. Remember when you were a kid playing on the playground and you hopped on the teeter-totter with a friend? When you went up, your friend went down, and vice versa. And there was always one kid who used to get you up in the air and hold you there, right?

Faith and disappointment ride on opposite sides of a teeter-totter. On one side of the teeter-totter are our faith, hopes, dreams, and expectations, but on the other side are our life's disappointments. When our disappointments rise, our faith, hopes, dreams, and expectations fall (see Figure 3).

FIGURE 3

You must process your disappointments to develop deep faith. If you allow your disappointments to go unprocessed, your faith will be unfruitful. Often when we are disappointed, we struggle to trust God. We feel hurt and take offense at God; we wonder why God didn't come through for us. Unprocessed disappointment causes us to close down our hearts. We shut down our hearts so that we will not be hurt any more.

Proverbs 13:12 says, "Hope deferred makes the heart sick, but a longing fulfilled is a tree of life." When we are longing for something, hoping for some person to be healed, or to come to Christ, or a dream to be fulfilled, or a child to walk in the fullness of Christ, and it doesn't happen, our hearts get hurt. We become sick at heart and soul. Unless we process that heart disease, our faith will be hindered.

The problem is that our faith, hopes, dreams, and expectations are directly tied to our passions. These are the things that we believe deeply in, care preeminently about, and live strenuously for. When our hopes are dashed, our passions get displaced. Displaced passions are dangerous to the soul and to the journey of deep faith. Sometimes they run to unholy passions, and sometimes they are snuffed out and we settle for something very different from the good life God intends for us.

If we are going to reawaken our passions, we must process our disappointments. I think most midlife crises are really just accumulated disappointments. Our life is good, but not as good as we had hoped; our marriage is good, but we aren't as close as we had dreamed; our finances are sufficient, but we aren't where we expected to be; our kids are good kids, but they aren't all in for Jesus; our career and calling are good, but we aren't making the impact we thought we would. And the things we dreamed about when we were twenty have not come about as we hoped. We are disappointed, and we end up with displaced passions that lead us to a midlife crisis and an affair or running out to buy a sports car or some other symbolic expense to try to reignite our passion. We know something is missing, but we don't know what or how. We have to process our disappointments.

Here are just a couple of thoughts about processing disappointments. First, be sure to process, and not just talk about, your disappointments. So many times people get stuck because they are not processing; they are just talking. If you are talking about the same things over and over, but not making any progress, you are likely just talking and not processing. When I get stuck in talking, I have my eyes on my circumstances, on myself, and on my lack of resources to break through. But when I genuinely process with God, I talk about all of those things, and I make an intentional effort to look up to God. I take my eyes off myself, my lack of resources, and my circumstances, and I lift my eyes to God. I grab hold of my lifelines, and I intentionally remember the goodness of God.

I love the psalmists because they are masterful at grieving their losses, accessing their deep emotion, processing their pain, and looking up to God in faith-filled surrender. Until I look up and out of myself—up toward God—I cannot process.

Again, we need to express our hearts honestly to God. This is vital for developing deep trust. Burying pain only breeds distrust. Often we use religious slogans to mask our pain: "God is good, all the time"; or, "God works everything for good." The problem isn't with the accuracy of these statements; the problem is when our hearts are not in alignment with the reality of what they truly mean. God doesn't want us to throw around religious slogans and cover up our pain and distrust. God wants us to authentically process our pain and disappointments so we can arrive at a place of deep faith.

I love praying the Psalms because they don't shrink from emotional displays and honest expression; they are raw but reverent, honest but honorable. For example, Psalm 13:1, 2 says: "How long, Lord? Will you forget me forever? How long must I wrestle with my thoughts and day after day have sorrow in my heart?" Psalm 38:8-10: "I am feeble and utterly crushed; I groan in anguish of heart. All my longings lie open before you, Lord; my sighing is not hidden from you. My heart pounds, my strength fails me; even the light has gone from my eyes."

They let it all out. We live in a broken, fallen world, and there is a lot of pain and disappointment that accumulates in a lifetime. We must get it up and out of our inner being or it festers in our heart like a poison.

I have often joked that if my children ever publish my journals after I die, like I've seen some people do, I will come back and haunt them. My journals are intimate expressions of my disappointments, griefs, sorrows, hurts, and letdowns in life. Of course, there are many good things that I celebrate, and they are filled with thanksgiving as well. But, like the Psalms, they often sound a bit schizophrenic. "Oh, God, how could you allow this? Where are you? Why did you not come to my rescue? I'm hurt and abandoned." But have you ever noticed how the Psalms end? They all eventually come to surrender: "But, I love you. You are good. I trust you. You will deliver me. I surrender." They sound a bit emotionally unsteady at times, but that is the honest life of deep faith. We have to process our disappointments to develop deep faith.

Be careful in these times to guard against misplaced passions. See Psalm 141:1-4:

> I call to you, Lord, come quickly to me; hear me when I call to you. May my prayer be set before you like incense; may the lifting up of my hands be like the evening sacrifice.

> Set a guard over my mouth, Lord; keep watch over the door of my lips.

> Let not my heart be drawn to what is evil so that I take part in wicked deeds along with those who are evildoers; let me not eat their delicacies.

This is brilliant advice from a master soul keeper. David knew that in the dark valleys, when his disappointments were high, he was more susceptible to misplaced passion. He was more tempted to say things he would regret, and to act out in anger, grumbling, and complaining against the Lord and quenching of the Spirit. So he prays that God would put a watch over his mouth. He knew he was more likely to fall prey to unholy passions in an effort to rekindle a flame deep within him, to regain some of the life that has been lost at the center of his soul, so he prays that his heart may not be drawn to what is evil. He was a master of the soul.

The more passionate you are, the more disappointments you will suffer. Passionate people have higher expectations. Many of your aspirations will not be met, so you must process your disappointments with God in order to reawaken your holy hopes and passions.

I have been the pastor of South Shore Community Church (SSCC) for more than twenty years, and in June of 2017, I will leave SSCC and become a full-time faculty member at Alliance Theological Seminary. I started the church when I was thirty, and when I envisioned the church back then I thought we would be in a far different place than we are as I depart. I anticipated we would have seen a full-blown revival by now; after all, I had promises along these lines, along with a sign that was fulfilled. I have spent many long hours in my journal processing my disappointments so I could rekindle my holy passions and avoid misplaced passions. It has been vital to my journey and exceedingly important to the development of my faith. In the end, if we can process our disappointments, we can get our eyes off ourselves and back on God. If we can express our hearts fully, and surrender ourselves completely to God, we will strengthen our intimacy and deepen our faith.

Fight to keep your heart soft. Hope deferred cannot only make the heart sick, it can make the heart hard. Proverbs 4:23 says, "Above all else, guard your heart, for it is the wellspring of life" (NIV 1984).

We must guard our hearts. Guarding our hearts is not about self-protection. It is about guarding the *condition* of our hearts. Often, we put up shields to protect our hearts from pain. The problem with shields is that they are indiscriminate; not only do they block out the people and things in our life that are trying to hurt us, they block out God from healing us.

Guarding our hearts means that we fight to keep our hearts soft, broken, humble, and contrite before God. We remember his love; we give thanks for all good things; we recall that God redeems all things to make us more like Jesus; and we surrender to a good Father who can be trusted.

I battled discouragement for two years. Every day I woke up and had to fight against it. I would overcome most days, but the next morning when I woke up, the black cloud was back, and I had to fight against it again. I felt like I was drowning. I was doing all the right things. I had forgiven those who had sinned against me, I had journaled through all my disappointments and grieved all my losses. I was ruthlessly honest with God and others, and I continually surrendered and gave thanks. I practiced worship regularly and continued to faithfully spend time with God and pursue Him as my first love and first pursuit.

But I was locked in a battle I could not win. I might rise above the discouragement for a week or two, but it kept coming back. One day I was in my backyard talking to God about it. I said, "Lord, this is the first time in my life I have not been able to surrender my way through an issue. Every other time in my life I have been able to surrender, and the issue would lift. Why can't I surrender my way through this issue?"

As I prayed that day I had a revelation: I was trying to surrender a symptom, and I wasn't dealing with the disease. Discouragement was only a symptom. I went inside and shared the insight with Jen. I prayed for the Lord to show me the root of the discouragement. About a week later I was talking with Jen about the issues at church that were weighing so heavily on me, issues of discouragement. I said to her, "I feel like I am wasting my life." As soon as the words came from my mouth, I knew that was the root. I said, "That's it! That's the root of my discouragement." That moment I surrendered it to the Lord.

I remember when I first came to New England. I was

talking with another pastor who had been in the District a long time, and he was sharing his call to New England with me. His call came from Ezekiel: "You are not being sent to a people of obscure speech and strange language, whose words you cannot understand. Surely if I had sent you to them, they would have listened to you. But the people of Israel are not willing to listen to you because they are not willing to listen to me" (Ezekiel 3:5-7).

I remember leaving that conversation and saying to Jen, "That is the worst calling ever. The worst calling that I could think of is the call to live a fruitless life ministering to a stiff-necked people who will never respond."

I never wanted to live a life that felt fruitless, and that was exactly how I was feeling. It wasn't about the people at SSCC, it was about the region of New England. It wasn't that we weren't seeing good things; we saw many people saved, healed, delivered, and transformed. It was about not seeing all the things I had dreamed. It was about not seeing the amount of fruit I had imagined.

New England was a notoriously hard and unresponsive region. And that was the root of my discouragement. I felt as though had I chosen to go to a different place, a different region, I would have borne more fruit; we would have seen more people saved, healed, delivered, and transformed.

But once I surrendered it, the discouragement lifted. I repented of my frustration and my false motivations, and I surrendered to the King. That day the teeter-totter shifted—disappointment got less weighty in my life, and faith rose and triumphed.

Faith is simply taking God at his word. It is an active trust in the goodness of the Father. Deep faith is cultivated in closeness to God. But if you are going to draw near and develop the intimacy with God that fosters deep faith, then you must embrace the process of purging, cleansing, pruning, and unpacking your disappointments.

It isn't easy or pleasant to welcome the pruning work of the Spirit in your life, but it is worth it, and it is utterly essential for the deep faith necessary to see the works of the Kingdom.

Reflection Questions

1. Do you have any disappointments you have allowed to accumulate in your soul, experiences you have not fully processed and unpacked? Take a moment to reflect. Ask God to show you if there are any areas that need deeper processing.

2. Do you intentionally engage in fighting for your trust by focusing on the cross, on Jesus, to solidify your faith? Pay attention to your self-talk. What runs through your mind in times of crisis and hardship? What do you feel? What do you think? Are you intentionally combatting thoughts of distrust?

3. Have you resolved to spend time with God through thick and thin?

4. Is there anything you need to surrender to God to solidify your faith?

5. Which of the three trust barriers—sin, fear, and disappointments—is most detrimental to your faith right now? Why? What can you do to intentionally engage in overcoming that obstacle and develop deep faith?

Four:
Feed Your Faith

*"Every experience God gives us,
every person He puts in our lives, is the perfect
preparation for the future that only He can see."*

—Corrie ten Boom

*"Reading, meditating on, and praying Scripture has brought
light into my darkest moments, strength to my weakness, hope
to my despair, enough to my 'too little,' living water to my barren soul, and an eternal perspective to my temporal problems."*

—Rob Reimer

I love fire. We have two fireplaces in our home, and they
were a big selling point for me. I have a portable metal fire
pit in my yard that I drag out and use frequently. I love the
mystery and power of fire; I love watching fire burn, feeling its
heat, experiencing the peaceful feeling it brings.

But, of course, you have to feed a fire or it stops burning.

A couple of winters back we had a severe storm that
knocked out our power for several days. We all camped in the

living room around the fireplace. Day and night, I kept the fire burning to keep us warm. I had to get up multiple times each night to feed the fire because it was our only source of heat.

Faith is not unlike a fire; you must feed your faith, just like a fire, to keep it burning. When I read Matthew 10 some years ago, and had a revelation about the deficiencies in my faith, I realized that I could not be passive about it. I had to intentionally develop my faith; I had to feed my faith like I have to feed a fire with logs. Let's look at some of the resources available to us to feed our faith.

Scripture

The first book we turn to for the feeding of faith is the Bible. Scripture is filled with demonstrations of the faithfulness of God to his people and the revelations of God, his ways, and his doings. Reading these accounts fill our hearts with faith.

I have been strengthened in my pursuit of God by studying the life of Moses, who overcame his shame and became a face-to-face friend of God. I have been steadied in times of testing by saturating myself in the life of David, who endured a long season of trials before the promise of the kingship was delivered to him. My faltering faith was greatly reinforced by meditating on Hebrews 11 and seeing how these great saints lived for the promises of God, even when those promises were not fulfilled until a future generation. Reading, meditating on, and praying Scripture has brought light into my darkest moments, strength to my weakness, hope to my despair, enough to my 'too little,' living water to my barren soul, and an eternal perspective to my temporal problems.

I have read the Bible from cover to cover at least once every year for the past thirty-five years. I have studied the lives of great saints from the pages of Scripture and been encouraged that what God did for them, He could and would do for me. I have meditated on a snippet of Scripture, like Psalm 23, nearly daily for months on end, and it has fed my soul and steadied my anxious heart, allowing me to trust God in difficult circumstances. I have prayed the promises of God, like Romans 8:28—that God would redeem whatever comes my way to make me more like Jesus. Every time circumstances arose that threatened to snuff out the flame of faith in my heart, God stoked the fire once again with Scripture. Every time you pick up the Bible, you are one Holy Spirit breath away from a fresh encounter with the living God. So, over and over again, I have turned to this holy book for divine encounters, supernatural revelation, and Holy Spirit inspiration.

> Every time you pick up the Bible, you are one Holy Spirit breath away from a fresh encounter with the living God.

You must learn to feed your soul, and your faith, with the Scriptures. God has chosen to reveal Himself to us in these pages, and we must go there often. The purpose of reading the Bible isn't to know the Bible; the purpose of reading the Bible is to *know* God. It isn't an end in itself; it is a means to an end. It is not designed to point us to its pages, but to point us to God Himself.

In these pages of revelation, our trust in our good Father can be forged and strengthened, rekindled and reinforced. Ultimately, faith is simply taking God at his word. We trust what He has recorded for us in the pages of Scripture, and we trust what He is revealing to us through our personal interactions with Him. But even these promptings of the Spirit, these personal revelations from God, must be tested by the Word of God. This is the starting point on our road to deep faith.

Praying the promises of God found in Scripture has been a vital part of strengthening my faith. 1 John 5:14, 15 says: "This is the confidence we have in approaching God: that if we ask anything according to his will, he hears us. And if we know that he hears us—whatever we ask—we know that we have what we asked of him."

We can pray anything according to God's will, and He will do it. This is a key promise to praying in faith: Find what God wants, and then pray it until it comes. When I am praying for something I know is God's will, I often recall this promise and claim it. If I can find a promise in Scripture to lay hold of, I will pray that with tenacity, because I know that if I pray according to God's will, He will hear me and do it.

For example, Jesus promised us peace, his peace. In John 14:27 He says, "Peace I leave with you; my peace I give you. I do not give to you as the world gives. Do not let your hearts be troubled and do not be afraid." The peace of Jesus is rooted in eternity; He is seated on His throne in heaven today, and He isn't nervous. So when anxiety threatens to rob me of my peace, when worries about the future disrupt the peace of the present, I claim this promise and hold on to it in faith. I wait on God and listen to Him for wisdom from the Holy Spirit, because I believe He has peace that He wants to impart to me, and I believe He knows how to get to the depths of my soul. I will seek Him and wait for Him to reveal to me any blocks to his peace, any action steps I must take on the road to his peace, and I will claim that peace until it is restored to me. I can pray any promise of God with absolute certainty according to 1 John 5:14, 15: we know He hears us when we are praying his promises back to Him. We must, of course, correctly interpret and apply the promises, and we must persist. But if God said it, God will do it.

Other Books

When I realized my faith for healing was lagging, I took

intentional action steps to build my faith by reading books on healing. I went back and reread some classics like A.B. Simpson's *The Gospel of Healing* and *The Fourfold Gospel* and Andrew Murray's book, *Divine Healing*. I read modern books on healing, mostly written by my charismatic brothers and sisters, because, sadly, there aren't too many modern books on healing written by those from my Evangelical tradition.

I also saturated my soul with books on prayer from many ancient and modern writers. I reread all of E.M Bounds's works on prayer. I read books on prayer by Andrew Murray, A.B. Simpson, George Muller, Charles Finney, John Wesley, R.A. Torrey, and others. I also read biographies of great saints who saw the supernatural interventions of God in their lives and ministries. These writers served to inspire me and instruct me; they strengthened and enriched my faith. The important point is not what I read; there was no magic in that alone. The important point is I was intentionally engaging in the development of my faith.

You cannot sit back passively and wait for faith to magically appear. You may grow older and not wiser; you may grow up in years but not in faith. I didn't want time to pass by while I sat around passively waiting for God to do something I was responsible for. I took responsibility to develop my faith, and reading was a key tool in my developmental process.

Testimonies

I began to collect and recollect testimonies that fed the fire of my faith. Revelation 19:10 says, "For the testimony of Jesus is the Spirit of prophecy." When you hear a testimony of Jesus' power, Jesus' victory, Jesus' deliverance, Jesus' healing, or Jesus' redeeming work in another person's life, it inspires faith to believe Him for that same thing in your own life.

I went through my prayer journal and recalled healing stories I had witnessed. I rejoiced over them again, and I retold them to myself and others. I read the testimonies of others in the books I read. I watched some healing testimonies on videos and YouTube. I asked people about healing stories they had experienced. Again, these were intentional steps in the developmental process of faith.

You can fix your mind on your problems, or you can fix your mind on Jesus and his solutions. If you fix your mind on your problems, you will feed fear and anxiety, and you will snuff out the fire of faith. But if you fix your mind on the testimony of Jesus and his power, you will feed the fire of faith in your soul.

> You can fix your mind on your problems, or you can fix your mind on Jesus and his solutions.

I was ashamed to discover how many stories I had forgotten of Jesus' miraculous interventions and supernatural displays of power. If the testimony of Jesus works like currency, then He had given me great resources to work with. Sadly, rather than depositing them in the bank of my memory so they could collect interest, I laid them down and forgot them, much like an uncashed check.

If you want to develop faith, you must cash the check of Jesus' testimony and deposit it in the bank of your memory so it can collect interest and return to you as deep faith. I went back and recovered stories of healing in my family, in the church, and in my own life.

Years ago, I saw a woman healed in Ecuador; she got up out of a wheelchair and walked. I tell that story in my book *Soul Care*. But that night I saw another miracle. What I didn't tell in that book is that when I prayed for this woman, I was as sick as I have ever been. I had eaten some fish soup that made me horribly ill. I hadn't eaten anything in days when I prayed for that woman in the wheelchair, not because I was fasting, but because I was too sick to eat.

That night, we went up on the mountaintop in Quito, and I was celebrating what had happened with a friend. I said to him, "You know what's funny? I've actually never personally experienced a healing before in my own life." Right after I said that, I heard the Spirit whisper in my inner being, "Do you want to? Lay your hand on your stomach as you walk, and pray for healing." I did, and instantly I felt better. I went out for dinner that night and ate barbeque. All my Ecuadorian friends who had seen how sick I was for the past few days tried to talk me out of eating barbeque, but I knew I was healed. And it was delicious!

A few years ago, at the close of our District Conference, which is where all the pastors come together in the New England District of the Christian and Missionary Alliance, I was on the prayer team. We were praying for the sick and for anyone who came forward for special prayer.

I teamed with Chris Wilkens, a Christian counselor and friend, and we prayed for a few people for various things. We didn't see anything visible happen at the time we prayed, however. I see many of these pastors only once a year, at our District Conference, so I didn't hear a report on what happened until the following year.

At the next District Conference, a man approached me as soon as I arrived. He said, "Last year you prayed for me at District Conference. Do you remember?" It started coming back to me. He said, "You prayed for my shoulder. It had hurt for decades. It hurt for one more day, and it hasn't hurt since. God healed my shoulder."

I said, "Praise God! That's awesome." He said, "Wait. I'm not done. You also prayed for my house to sell. It had been on the market for a long time and no one was interested in it. It sold right after District Conference."

I said, "That's awesome." He said, "Wait. I'm not done. You also prayed for me because I have been a widower for a long time, and I have been lonely." He beamed. And he took the hand of the woman next to him and said, "Let me introduce you to my new wife."

> All of God's workings are part of our history because we have been adopted into his family. Every story we hear, every miracle we read about, every healing we witness, every testimony in the Bible, is an opportunity for us to throw another log on the fire of our faith.

I laughed and said, "That was a heck of a prayer time!" He said, "I've had some pretty cool God experiences in my life, but that topped them all."

That story flooded my soul with faith, and when I prayed for people that year at District Conference, I came full of expectancy in what God would do. He delivered with another miraculous healing as I prayed for a man with vertigo.

All of God's workings are part of our history because we have been adopted into his family. Every story we hear, every miracle we read about, every healing we witness, every testimony in the Bible, is an opportunity for us to throw another log on the fire of our faith. These are our family stories; they are part of our birthright as adopted children of our heavenly Father.

I have always loved getting together with my extended family, particularly when my grandparents were alive. I loved listening to our family stories; we told the same stories over and over, but they were part of our family legacy, our family heritage. They helped us recall who we were, and are, and what God had done in our midst. We laughed together and celebrated together God's goodness to us as a family. Faith got passed on through those conversations and stories.

This is the power of the testimony of Jesus, and every story of Jesus' powerful working is part of our family history. Own them. Internalize them. Collect them and recollect them to develop deep faith.

Experiences

I don't have many collections. I do have an old baseball card collection from when I was a kid. I have complete sets of Topps baseball cards from 1975 through somewhere in the 1990s. And I do have a cool hat collection. It has become a tradition of mine to buy a hat from every stadium I visit, and I have visited a lot of ballparks. But mostly what I collect are experiences. I love new experiences; I love traveling to new places, experiencing new things, eating new foods, visiting new sights.

Above all, I love collecting new God experiences. I love fresh new encounters with God that build and enrich my personal history with God. I love being on hand to see God do the works of the Kingdom afresh. When God revealed the weakness in my faith I have been writing about, I intentionally pursued new experiences that could expand my faith.

I went to several healing conferences, including one led by John Arnott. Sadly, I had heard a lot of negative, reactionary things about Arnott from some church people I knew. But I have discovered that fear-based reactions are seldom rooted in reality, and I have learned not to make a judgment on someone's life based on another person's opinion of them. Fear is a tool of the enemy to keep us from the fullness of God. And so often the church has fear about things of the Spirit; that isn't from Jesus. Jesus isn't afraid of the Holy Spirit or his miraculous workings.

I heard John give a talk on healing that could have been written by A.B. Simpson or Andrew Murray. It was Jesus-centered, biblically solid, and God-honoring. There was no flair or fancy, no self-promotion or self-aggrandizement. It was a simple, straightforward, Jesus-heals talk, and John added that healing is often blocked by unforgiveness. He asked people to stand who had been involved in accidents, asked them if they blamed anyone for their accident, and then led them through forgiveness.

People forgave everything from drunk drivers who left them in crippling back pain to negligent coworkers who caused them to experience a work accident. One woman forgave a cow that ran in front of her car and left her with a severe neck injury. Over and over as people forgave themselves and others—even a cow—they were prayed for and released from their pain. I watched hundreds of people get healed, and many of the healings were noticeable; you could see a visible change—like skin rashes disappearing. It was powerful to behold. I saw things that day I had never seen before.

Experiencing things we have never seen before can enlarge our faith. I went to several of these conferences, and they were useful. But after going to what was probably my third one, I was driving home and said to Jen, "I'm not going to any more of these conferences. I know the teaching. I believe the theology that Jesus heals. I've taught on it myself long before I even went to these conferences. I don't need to hear it any more. I have seen a lot of healings and I am grateful for that; that has been good. But I haven't been praying for the sick at these events myself, and I need to see things that I have never seen before. I need to go on a missions trip to one of these places where they are seeing a lot of healing, with one of these guys who God has used greatly in this ministry."

Shortly after I had spoken those words to Jen, I received an email from a person who said they felt prompted by the Spirit to send us twenty thousand dollars to send our family on a missions trip with Randy Clark to Brazil.

Again, I had heard a lot of negative press about Randy Clark, but I have also heard him speak on a variety of topics, and the teaching that I had heard was biblically solid and Jesus-centered. I hope I live to see the day when Christians stop fighting and attacking other Christians, and live in unity and charity on mission for the King. When we are battling in the trenches to set the captives of hell free from sin, bondage, and disrepair, it hardly seems appropriate to turn our weapons on fellow soldiers on the same mission for the same King. I love the axiom of John Wesley: "If you love Jesus, give me your hand and I'll work with you."

So I went to Brazil with my family, and I saw things I have never seen before. We saw a man who was born deaf and mute healed by Jesus, and he heard his mother's voice and spoke his first word: "Jesus." If seeing a miracle like that doesn't move a person to tears and awe of Jesus, it may be questionable if that person even has a heart.

I prayed for people all week long and saw all sorts of miracles. People who walked in limping and left leaping and praising God. People who had such back pain that they came in grimacing and left smiling and bending down to try and touch their toes. People who came in with such shoulder pain that they couldn't lift their hands over their heads, and left raising their hands to full extension in praise of Jesus the healer. I prayed with one elderly pastor's wife, who was stooped over with osteoporosis, and she straightened up before my eyes. When she bent over she couldn't straighten back up on her own; she needed her husband to help her. She just had to demonstrate for me, so she bent over and couldn't get back up. But, as I prayed for her in Jesus' name, she immediately straightened up and started bending over and reaching for her toes – up and down, up and down she went as tears of joy streamed down her face and she gave a shout of praise.

But I had seen these kinds of miracles before when I prayed for people, and while it was cool to see Randy and his team pray for a deaf-mute person who was healed, I wanted to be in on the action, and I wanted to see something I had never seen before.

The last day I was there, I said this to my team: I am only praying today for people with visible problems. No back aches or shoulder pains or stomach ailments. I want to see the blind see or the deaf hear or a tumor disappear, so I'm only praying for those types of people.

I spent nearly an hour praying for one man who was born blind, but he did not see.

I prayed with my oldest daughter, Danielle, for another woman blind from birth. We prayed for her for forty-five minutes; she had so many deep wounds, far deeper than the surface. She had been rejected by her family. We did not see her eyes opened, but her heart was deeply healed, and I watched my daughter minister to her with the tenderness of the Father.

But I did see something I had longed to see. A woman approached me who had a goiter on her neck. It was so large it extended past her chin. She was a thin woman, and she was obviously in discomfort. She faced travel of twenty-four hours just to reach a hospital that could help her, and even if she could have gotten there, she couldn't have afforded it.

She came with tears dripping down her cheeks, and she was trembling. She was desperate; she had no other options, no other solutions, no other hope. It was a Jesus miracle or a horrible goiter; there was no in-between.

I laid my hand on her goiter and simply prayed, "Go, in Jesus' name." And the goiter shrank under my hand. I said it a second time, and it shrank the rest of the way as her body returned to normal. She and her husband cried and threw their arms around me; they spoke in rapid-fire Portuguese, but I had no translator and didn't understand a word of it. I'll have to wait till Heaven to get the translation, but I could guess at their words. Only Jesus.

My friend Ron Walborn says, "God doesn't want to be the God of the last resort. He wants to be the God of the first defense." So often He is the God of the last resort for those of us in the Western world. We run to the medicine cabinet and to the doctor's office looking for solutions to what ails us, rather than running to God. Only in turning to God, and seeing God do what God alone can do, can we expand our faith.

I have heard people say to me, "I won't travel to see God work. Why can't God work here? If God wants to do a miracle, He can do it here. Why should I have to travel?" Imagine if those in the Gospels had that attitude. Imagine if they were unwilling to travel to go where Jesus was working; imagine what miracles would have been left untold.

Sometimes our stubbornness exceeds our desire for more, and our narrowness keeps us from expanding our faith. Go where you need to go. Expand your boundaries, expand beyond your theological camp to other Christ-centered camps, and expand your experiences with God. If you get outside your normal church experience, don't be surprised if you feel uncomfortable. Another Ron Walborn line is apropos: too often "people confuse discernment with their comfort zone." *Just because it is outside your comfort zone doesn't make it outside of God's realm of possibilities.* Authentic discernment cannot happen without expanding the boundaries of our comfort zone to the size of God's comfort zone. Fear often keeps us from increasing our experiences and expanding our faith. That isn't discernment; that is just sad.

Risk

Sooner or later you have read all the books you need to

read, heard all the testimonies you need to hear, and collected all the experiences you need to collect. It is at that point that you just need to dive in.

You can't expand faith without shifting from observing to doing, and that shift requires risk. It is always more comfortable and safer to watch someone else do the works of the Kingdom than it is to risk trusting God in Kingdom action.

I was twenty-five years old when I did my first deliverance, and I had never seen a deliverance successfully done, but someone had to do it. There was a woman in need, the Lord was able, and I was willing—that was all that was needed to shift from observing to doing. The young woman got free, and my faith got developed. Your next level with God lies beyond the boundaries of your current experience, and the only way you can get there is to risk more than you are comfortable with.

> Your next level with God lies beyond the boundaries of your current experience, and the only way you can get there is to risk more than you are comfortable with.

When you take a risk, you get out and beyond your comfort zone, and you take new territory. It is like learning a new skill. At first, when you learn a new skill, it feels awkward and unnatural. But the more you practice it, the more you engage in that new skill set, the more you develop a comfort. You expand your comfort zone—what was once uncomfortable and unnatural has now become comfortable and natural.

This is true in experiencing John 14:12 realities. When I first started hearing God's promptings, it was most unnatural for me to take a risk and do anything with it. I faltered and hesitated because I was uncertain. I questioned: "Is that really God? How do I know?" But I risked, and in so doing, I expanded my comfort zone.

It was like a toddler learning to walk: I stumbled and fell and made plenty of beginner's mistakes. But I also discovered God is really gracious, and most people are pretty gracious, too. Eventually, what started as something very awkward and uncomfortable became something very naturally supernatural. It became my new norm.

I have learned to trust the promptings of the Spirit implicitly—not without testing it with humility—but I don't hesitate to bring forth what I believe God is whispering to me and test it. It has become so natural for me to operate with faith in this area of hearing God that I often say, "I don't know how people do life without hearing God's voice."

This was equally true for me in the area of deliverance. When I first started helping people get free from the demonic, I was nervous and way beyond my comfort zone. There were times when demons manifested, and I could feel my soul cower within me. I can't begin to tell you how many times I was stumped and had no idea what to do.

But the stories I can tell, the freedom I've seen, the life change I've witnessed, has been remarkable. It has contributed to the testimony of Jesus that will be told through all eternity—and all it cost me was risky faith. All of that couldn't happen unless I risked more than I was comfortable with; all of that couldn't happen unless I was willing to develop faith by risking a venture into unknown spiritual territory.

So often what keeps us from experiencing the release of the promise of John 14:12 in our lives is the fear of stepping into unknown territory. We are afraid to take a risk. We are afraid that we might not know what to do. We are afraid that we might not have what it takes. We are afraid that we might not get it perfect, or worse, get it all wrong. We fear that we might blow it, embarrass ourselves, or lose face.

Let me help by taking the pressure off: You will blow it at

times, you will be in over your head, and you will not have what it takes or know what to do. *But Jesus isn't nervous. And He knows what to do.* Theology 101: God is smart, and He knows stuff we don't know, and He likes to tell us. We will never know what only God knows if we only do what we can already do. We will never see what only God can do if we only stay in our current comfort zone. Too often we make it too much about us and too little about God, and we see too much of our human limitations and too little of God's limitless possibilities.

> Faith is not deepened in the halls of academia; faith is deepened on the front lines of ministry that is dependent upon God showing up and doing what only God can do.

Get training on these John 14:12 areas that are beyond your current experience. Go to conferences, listen to testimonies, read books, and learn from others. But sooner or later, you have to dive into the deep end of the pool. You have to move from observing to acting, or you never develop faith.

Faith is not deepened in the halls of academia; faith is deepened on the front lines of ministry that is dependent upon God showing up and doing what only God can do. I started my risky faith with listening to the promptings of the Spirit and passing them along. (I have a chapter on how to hear God's voice in *River Dwellers*.) Then I expanded from there to other areas, like deliverance and healing. The great thing about faith risks is that each time you risk in one area, you develop your trust in God and gain the courage needed to risk in another area.

Obey

Disobedience disintegrates faith, but obedience develops faith. Obedience ultimately is all about trust. Do we trust God enough to surrender and accept his ways over our ways? For example, God tells us to forgive our enemies, but it doesn't seem right or fair to us. Will we trust God enough to believe that He knows stuff we don't know and simply obey Him? When we obey God, we discover that God is trustworthy. When we disobey God, it erodes our faith.

> The opposite of faith is not doubt. The opposite of faith is unbelief, and the fruit of unbelief is disobedience.

When I was in my doctoral program, Haddon Robinson, my professor, used to say, "The opposite of faith is not doubt; the opposite of faith is disobedience." I love that statement, but I would state it slightly differently. The opposite of faith is not doubt. The opposite of faith is unbelief, and the fruit of unbelief is disobedience.

For example, Jesus told us to forgive those who sin against us. We may agree to forgive our enemies, yet still doubt that this path is going to be most beneficial. We may agree to forgive, but still be fearful that it is going to come back to hurt us. So we launch out with fear and trembling on the legs of wobbly faith, and we agree with God to forgive; we make a conscious decision to let the offense go, to no longer rehearse it or review it. We decide to take Jesus literally and pray blessings on our enemies, to pray good things for their lives.

Our faith may be weak and wobbly as we start down this road, but we start—and that is faith mingled with doubt. We stay the course: we keep agreeing to forgive, we keep praying blessings, we keep resolving not to bring up the offense.

And one day a miracle happens: God does what only God can do. He changes our heart. We find our anger and hurt and bitterness is supernaturally replaced by his love. We did what we could do, we took God at his Word, we obeyed Him with all our human frailty, and God did what we couldn't do: He changed our heart.

After an experience like that, the next time we get hurt, we will move forward in obedience to forgive with much greater confidence in the outcomes, with much deeper trust in God. Obedience develops faith.

The first time God gave me a prophetic prompting of the Spirit for someone else, I did not plunge headlong into it with great confidence. I prayed about it and asked God for assurance. I waited on it and reluctantly tottered forward with fear and trembling. But when I gave the word and the person was moved to tears because the word landed, my faith was strengthened. Taking the risk to obey God was like throwing another log on the fire of my faith.

Corrie ten Boom, who was an evangelist for the Lord after surviving the Nazi concentration camps, said, "When we are powerless to do a thing, it is a great joy that we can come and step inside the ability of Jesus." That's what obedient faith does: it steps inside the ability of Jesus. We step out in obedience, and Jesus steps in to supply the power. But we won't see the power supplied unless we step out in faith.

Often, we wait for God to make us feel like doing something, or to change our hearts, before we launch out in obedient faith. God calls us to step out in trusting faith first, and then He promises the supply of all we need. The supply of God is never released to the apprehensive sideline watcher.

President Theodore Roosevelt (1901-1909) was known for his immense courage. These quotes inspire me to take risks for Jesus.

In 1899 Roosevelt said, "Far better to dare mighty things,

to win glorious triumphs, even though checkered by failure, than to take rank with those poor spirits who neither enjoy much nor suffer much, because they live in the gray twilight that knows not victory nor defeat."[9]

Then in 1910 Roosevelt expanded that quote: "It is not the critic who counts; not the man who points out how the strong man stumbles or where the doer of deeds could have done them better. The credit belongs to the man who is actually in the arena, whose face is marred by dust and sweat and blood; who strives valiantly; who errs, and comes short again and again, because there is no effort without error and shortcoming; but who does actually try to do the deeds; who knows the great enthusiasm, the great devotions, who spends himself in a worthy cause; who at the best knows in the end the triumph of high achievement, and who at worst, if he fails, at least fails while daring greatly, so that his place shall never be with those cold and timid souls who know neither victory nor defeat."[10]

Your next level with God lies beyond the boundaries of your current experience. The only way you can get there is to risk more than you are comfortable with. Get in the arena of risk, where deep faith is forged.

Reflection Questions

1. Are you intentionally developing your faith, or are you too passive about it? If you are intentional about developing your faith, how are you going about it?

2. Which of these tools have fed your faith in the past: Scripture, books, testimonies, experiences, risk, obedience? How?

---

9 Roosevelt, Theodore. *The Strenuous Life,* New York: Century Company, 1900, p. 6
10 Roosevelt, Theodore. Excerpt from the speech Citizens In a Republic, delivered at the Sorbonne in Paris on April 23, 1910

3. What tools are you using now to feed your faith: Scripture, books, testimonies, experiences, risk, obedience?

4. Which tools do you need to access to feed your faith? Why?

5. Is your current approach to reading Scripture deepening your faith? If you are not noticeably seeing your faith expand, how could you approach Scripture differently and feed your faith?

6. Talk to your friends about which books have expanded their faith. Which books would help you feed your faith?

7. What stories have you heard that inspired faith in you? What experiences have you had that inspired your faith? Have you shared your testimonies with others to feed their faith?

8. What risk is God calling you to take?

9. Where has obedience expanded your faith and deepened your trust? Is there any area in your life right now in which God is calling you to obey?

Five:
Testing, Humility, and Faith

"To learn strong faith is to endure great trials. I have learned my faith by standing firm amid severe testings."

—GEORGE MULLER

*"Pride isn't just the opposite of humility;
it is the paralysis of faith."*

—ROB REIMER

*"Humility is the simple disposition
which prepares the soul for living trust."*

—ANDREW MURRAY

You cannot develop deep faith without cultivating authentic humility. Andrew Murray, in his book *Humility*, makes the necessary link between humility and faith. Murray writes: "We need only think for a moment what faith is. Is it not the confession of nothingness and helplessness, the surrender and the waiting to let God work? Is it not in itself the most humbling thing there can be—the acceptance of our place as dependents, who can claim or get or do nothing but what grace bestows? Humility is simply the disposition which prepares the soul for living trust."[11]

Empty hands. Humility is all about the realization that we have nothing. We are lost and cannot save ourselves, so we hold up empty hands with faith in a merciful Savior to forgive our sins and reconcile us to God.

We are the only ones responsible for our lives, yet there are areas of brokenness and sin from which we cannot break free, so we hold up empty hands in faith while depending on the Spirit for victory. We are commissioned by Jesus to carry out the works of his Kingdom, yet we cannot change a heart or save a life or free a captive or force a demon to leave or heal a sick person or mend a soul, so we hold up empty hands in faith, looking to Jesus alone to do the works of the Kingdom through us. This is humility and faith.

Pride isn't just the opposite of humility; it is the paralysis of faith. Murray writes: "Pride renders faith impossible. Salvation comes through a cross and a crucified Christ. Salvation is the fellowship with the crucified Christ in the spirit of his cross. Salvation is union with and delight in, salvation is participation in, the humility of Jesus. Is it wonder that our faith is so feeble when pride still reigns so much, and we have scarce learnt even to long or pray for humility as the most needful and blessed part of salvation?"[12]

Pride makes everything too much about us; it leaves us feeling like we may have something in our hands or up our sleeves after all. Pride takes our eyes off of God, and calls us to rely on ourselves, look to ourselves, and trust in ourselves. Pride drives us to work harder and pray less; it pushes us to calculate

11 Murray, Andrew. *Humility*, Los Angeles, CA: IndoEuropean Publishing, 2009, p.58
12 Murray, Andrew. *Humility*, Los Angeles, CA: IndoEuropean Publishing, 2009, p.59

more and risk less. Pride causes us to rely more on our plans and less on his power; it results in us doing only what we can do with our best efforts, and yet never trusts God to do what only God can do through his power in our weakness. Pride causes us to create theologies that justify our spiritual impotence, and to excuse ourselves from the passages that call us to trust the Father for his mighty and miraculous interventions. Pride snuffs out the need for faith and makes the church about what *we* can do, accomplish, plan, or control. Pride makes the church look like the world and not the Kingdom; it leaves us with our programs and robs us of his power. Pride never produces a John 14:12 lifestyle. We should hold up empty hands; in truth, we have nothing.

Again, only twice in Scripture does Jesus speak of great faith. Both times that He mentions great faith, it is being shown through someone who displays humility. Murray, once again, picks up this connection in his book: "Humility and faith are more nearly allied in Scripture than many know. See it in the life of Christ. There are two cases in which He spoke of a great faith. Had not the centurion, at whose faith He marveled, saying, 'I have not found so great faith, no, not in Israel!' spoken, 'I am not worthy that Thou shouldst come under my roof'? And had not the mother to whom He spoke, 'O woman, great is thy faith!' accepted the name of dog, and said, 'Yea, Lord, yet the dogs eat of the crumbs'? It is the humility that brings a soul to be nothing before God, that also removes every hindrance to faith, and makes it only fear lest it should dishonor Him by not trusting Him wholly."[13]

To recognize our emptiness is to look to God's fullness. To see God's greatness with revelatory clarity is to come in humble dependence upon Him for all we need and all He has.

---

13 Murray, Andrew. *Humility*, Los Angeles, CA: IndoEuropean Publishing, 2009, p.59

Developing Humility

If we are going to develop deep faith, we must cultivate humility. How is humility nurtured? Zephaniah gives us some wisdom about growing in humility: "Seek the Lord, all you humble of the land, you who do what he commands. Seek righteousness, seek humility" (Zephaniah 2:3).

Humility begins with seeking the Lord. When we seek Him, we acknowledge our limits, our need, and our dependence on God. And when we seek the Lord, our character is formed in God's presence.

Part of our character formation is the development of humility. Humility is the mother of all virtues, and when we are with God, He develops humility in us. 1 John 3:2 says, "We know that when Christ appears, we shall be like him, for we shall see him as he is." Seeing Jesus face to face, as He is, will finalize our spiritual formation process; we shall be like Him when we enter his presence fully. But the spiritual principle underneath this truth is that his presence forms our character. When we are with Him, we become like Him.

> When we strengthen pride, we weaken faith; pride feeds trust in ourselves and fosters distrust in God.

Humility is also developed through surrender and obedience. We have to say yes to God. When we bow our stiff neck, yield our will to God's will, surrender to God's desires, and obey Him, humility is forged in our inner being.

This is why Zephaniah links the humble with "you who do what he commands." Every time we rebel against God and go our own way, we act on and fortify pride in our life. And when we strengthen pride, we weaken faith; pride feeds trust in ourselves and fosters distrust in God. But when we surrender and obey, we strengthen humility and fuel our faith.

Zephaniah teaches us to seek humility along with righteousness. We are to seek to develop humility; we are to seek God for it. We need to pray for it, and we need to embrace every opportunity to develop it.

Intentionally developing humility means we need to lean into the plethora of opportunities we have to own our mistakes, confess our sins, apologize for our wrongdoings, rectify our unrighteous actions, and speak of our weaknesses and failures. Intentionally developing humility means we need to receive correction without defense, entertain criticism without justification, and look for the truth in what is levied against us, not the lies. It means we cannot afford to spin, justify, excuse, blame, or defend our sin, but we must own all that we are responsible to own. We must stand in the light with God and others, taking full responsibility for our life.

Only in the light can humility be developed. Our natural inclination will be to defend, justify, blame, excuse, and spin our sin, but each time we opt for those proud actions, we strengthen pride's grip on our core, and we snuff out another candle of faith burning within. Every time we refuse our natural inclination and humble ourselves with brokenhearted apologies, and request forgiveness, we throw another log on the fire of faith.

Trials

There is another important part to developing humility that we need to examine: trials forge humility. The apostle Paul makes an interesting statement in his speech to the Ephesian elders in Acts 20. He says in Acts 20:19, "I served the Lord with great humility and with tears and in the midst of severe testing by the plots of my Jewish opponents."

In this passage, Paul claims to have served God with humility, and not just humility, but great humility. I've heard people say that if you claim you're humble, you are actually proud. But that wasn't true for Paul. How can he claim to be humble? He was humble because he followed Jesus—no matter what. No matter the cost, no matter who opposed, no matter where it led, no matter the blood he had to shed, no matter the tears he had to cry, no matter the prisons he had to enter, no matter the hostile mobs he had to face. His humility was demonstrated in his surrender and obedience; it was proven by his walk in the light, and through honest confession. It was revealed through his genuine affections and tenderhearted compassion for all the churches he influenced. His humility was established upon his knees as he interceded with tears for the world to be saved. His humility was authenticated in the scars that marred his body.

Humility isn't claimed; it is lived.

Humility isn't claimed; it is lived. And Paul lived it. He lived it every time he blessed those who cursed him and loved those who hated him. He lived it every time he suffered for Jesus and called it an honor. He lived it when he rejoiced in a prison cell after taking a beating. He lived out humility when he preached to those who persecuted him so that they might be redeemed like he was. He served the Lord with great humility.

Where did this man of God develop this great humility? It was in the tears and the trials. Paul didn't start out as a humble man; his pride was demonstrated in his rebellion against Jesus and his hostility toward those who followed Jesus. His pride was clearly seen in his dependence upon his own righteousness and fulfillment of the law as a good Pharisee. His path to humility started when Jesus knocked him off his horse on the road to Damascus. He was blinded by a great light; the great light revealed Paul's smallness and Jesus' greatness. It left him blind for a few days, and this served as a prophetic symbol—though he was educated and intelligent, he was spiritually ignorant and arrogant. This rightsizing of Paul's opinion of himself and Jesus was the beginning of humility. Humility always begins with a correct opinion of ourselves and Jesus. We need Him, because apart from Him we can do nothing.

Paul had to continue responding to the work of God in his soul to develop humility. Paul's humility didn't end with the revelation of Jesus and blindness; God had a plan for this man of many talents and unrelenting passion.

When God called Paul as an apostle, he asked Ananias to go and pray for him. Ananias had heard about Paul's abusive treatment to his fellow believers, so he was naturally reluctant to go! But God convinced him with these words: "Go! This man is my chosen instrument to proclaim my name to the Gentiles and their kings and to the people of Israel. I will show him how much he must suffer for my name" (Acts 9:15, 16).

> Trial, so often, is the crucible for the advancement of humility in the soul. No one develops humility without testing and tears, without triumph in trials.

Paul's calling included suffering, and his suffering forged his humility. Trial, so often, is the crucible for the advancement of humility in the soul. No one develops humility without testing and tears, without triumph in trials.

James discusses the importance of trials in James 1:2-4. "Consider it pure joy, my brothers and sisters, whenever you face trials of many kinds, because you know that the testing of your faith produces perseverance. Let perseverance finish its work so that you may be mature and complete, not lacking anything."

God tests us to refine us, complete us, perfect us. James goes on to distinguish between testing and temptation. "When tempted, no one should say 'God is tempting me.' For God cannot be tempted by evil, nor does he tempt anyone; but each person is tempted when they are dragged by their own evil desire and enticed. Then, after desire has conceived, it gives birth to sin; and sin, when it is full-grown, gives birth to death" (James 1:13-15).

God does not tempt us to stray from Him or to do evil. He has no evil in Him, and He cannot tempt another to do evil deeds. God tests us. Testing is different; the purpose of testing is not to hurt, to harm, or to create negative results. The purpose of testing is to strengthen, to ensure that someone has what it takes for success.

Think about a road test. We give people road tests to make sure that they are not dangerous to others or themselves when they drive. But the purpose of the road test isn't to fail people, or make it difficult for people, but to ensure their safety and the safety of others. When God tests us, He tests us to ensure we have what it takes to fulfill his eternal purposes for our lives.

When I was in college I took a lot of upper-level math courses. The teachers would explain the concepts in one unit, and then they would give you a test. Often the next unit would build off that previous unit, and after you completed the second unit, you would get another test. The ultimate purpose of these mid-course tests was to ensure you could master the difficult math so you would do well on the final and demonstrate your expertise.

My favorite college professor was a man who taught me differential equations. He came in the first day of class and announced, "Here is the final exam," as he proceeded to hand exam papers out to us. Then he went on: "I'll change the numbers, but these are the problems you will basically get. My job is to teach you how to do this so you can get an A. Your job is to learn so you can get an A."

He went on to explain that he wanted everyone in the class to achieve an A. He wasn't aiming for a bell curve; he was aiming for total mas-

> God is the master teacher; He wants every student to master the tests He sends so they become experts in living out this Kingdom life.

tery. For the first time in my life, I had a teacher who understood the purpose of education. The purpose of education is not so the teacher can impress the students with his or her mastery; the purpose of education is that students learn and master the subject themselves. God is the master teacher; He wants every student to master the tests He sends so they become experts in living out this Kingdom life.

Our job is to learn the test material as it comes along and ace the tests God sends our way so we can fulfill our prophetic destiny. James makes it clear to us that God doesn't leave us alone and bewildered in this time of testing. If we are going through a time of testing, and we cannot figure out why we are going through it or how God can redeem it to help us become more like Jesus and fulfill our divine purpose, then we need to ask Him.

James writes, "If any of you lacks wisdom, you should ask God, who gives generously to all without finding fault, and it will be given to you" (James 1:5). This is God's promise. He will give you wisdom in your time of testing if you ask Him.

James goes on to say we must ask Him in faith, not doubting, but trusting. We often quote this passage when we are asking God for life wisdom—wisdom about a big decision like whether we should marry this person or take a new career opportunity. That is fine, but that is not what the passage is referring to. The context is about trials and how God can redeem them in our lives to perfect us, to mature us. And notice, very specifically, that these trials are testing our faith (James 1:3).

If you are going to live out your divine purpose and fulfill your God-given destiny to make an impact

If you are going to live out your divine purpose and fulfill your God-given destiny to make an impact for the Kingdom, to do the works of the Kingdom, then your faith must be tried, tested, refined, perfected, and proven.

for the Kingdom, to do the works of the Kingdom, then your faith must be tried, tested, refined, perfected, and proven. God tests you to strengthen your faith so you can develop intimacy and maturity in Christ, and so you can have what it takes to fulfill the works of the Kingdom and live a John 14:12 lifestyle.

If we could only capture this thought, and live into it, imagine the difference it would make when we went through hardship.

George Muller, who lived so long on the certainty side of the faith spectrum, understood this concept and embraced it fully. Muller wrote, "If we, indeed, desire our faith to be strengthened, we should not shrink from opportunities where our faith may be tried, and, therefore, through the trial, be strengthened. In our natural state we dislike dealing with God alone . . . from depending on Him alone, from looking to Him alone . . . and yet this is the very position in which we ought to be, if we wish our faith to be strengthened."[14]

14 Muller, George. *Answers to Prayer,* Chicago, IL: Moody Press, 1984, p.36

That desire to trust ourselves, and not deal with God alone, is rooted in our pride. And only through the testing of our faith can pride be overcome and humility developed, and only in humility can we develop certain faith that trusts our Father in Heaven.

If we want to develop certain faith, we must embrace the testing. Yet, so often, we are pursuing God for more of Himself and more of his Kingdom, a trial comes our way, and the first thing we do is cry out for God to remove the trial. We ask God to take away the very thing He can redeem in our life to answer our original prayer for more of Him and more of his Kingdom. This is counterproductive to our spiritual well-being. We squirm under the weight of trials because we struggle to trust the intentions of our good Father.

> We squirm under the weight of trials because we struggle to trust the intentions of our good Father.

Redemptive Suffering

Understanding God's purpose behind testing does not, of course, take away from the pain of a trial, but it does strengthen us to endure the purpose of a trial. Someone once said we can endure any *how* if we know the *why*. If we know the purpose behind a trial, we have hope in the midst of the trial that God will see us through, redeem it, and bring great spiritual result on the other side of this difficulty. This was why George Muller suffered through such great material lack with such deep spiritual peace; Muller knew God was perfecting his faith so the Father could perform more miraculous works of the Kingdom through his life.

Think about this truth in light of Joseph's story. Joseph had a dream when he was a young man that he would be a ruler, lifted far above even his own family. Unwisely, and arrogantly, he shared his dream with his brothers, and they sold him up the river and into slavery. But the Lord was with Joseph; His favor rested upon the young man.

Joseph rose to a place of prominence in Potiphar's house. Please note: Joseph wasn't sold into slavery because God was punishing him or disappointed in him. God was forming Joseph into the man he needed to become to live out the dream God had for his life. God's favor rested on Joseph when He gave him the dream, and God's favor rested on Joseph when he was in slavery. Testing is not a sign of the lack of God's favor, but evidence of his favor.

However, Joseph was falsely accused of sexual harassment by Potiphar's wife, even though he behaved righteously, and he was imprisoned. Yet the Lord was with him in prison, and his favor once again rested on Joseph's life. Joseph rose to a place of prominence in the prison warden's eyes.

Eventually, through a supernatural interpretation of a dream (which is where the story began), Joseph is elevated to Pharaoh's second-in-command. When he stands before Pharaoh and the ruler recounts Joseph's ability to interpret dreams, Joseph says, "I cannot do it, but God will give Pharaoh the answer he desires."

This man who began with a divine destiny to rule for good was too proud to fulfill it, but the testing had refined the man, purified his pride, and left him with the deep humility to realize that he had empty hands but a good Father who could do all. Now he was prepared to step into his divine destiny.

This is the power of testing. Testing refines your character and deepens your intimacy with God so you can fulfill your divine purpose in life. If you take short cuts around the testing, your intimacy and character will not be prepared to handle power and success, and you will likely blow up your life in some dishonorable fashion.

This is why for years I prayed the prayer, "Lord, give me the ability to impart your Spirit, *if* my character and intimacy can sustain it." I wanted to see the Kingdom come. My heart longed to see revival, and I saw how the apostles laid hands on people and those people were filled with the Spirit.

No one performed miracles in the book of Acts until after the apostles laid hands on the deacons. Two of the deacons, Philip and Steven, became greatly known for their miracle-working ways. Acts 6:6 says that after they chose seven deacons as a new leadership level in the church, "They presented them to the apostles, who prayed and laid hands on them." Something was imparted in this laying on of hands.

Acts 6:8 says, "Now Stephen, a man full of God's grace and power, performed great wonders and signs among the people." Acts 8:6, 7 says Philip went to Samaria and preached about Jesus, and "When the crowds heard Philip and saw the signs he performed, they all paid close attention to what he said. For with shrieks, impure spirits came out of many, and many who were paralyzed or lame were healed."

When Jesus sent out the twelve and gave them authority over sickness and demons, He told them, "Freely you have received; freely give" (Matthew 10:8). They imparted the Spirit for healing, freedom, and miraculous release so that others would be filled with the Spirit, and for the imparting of spiritual gifts (e.g., Acts 6; Romans 1:11).

When they came and prayed, the Spirit manifested his presence, lives were changed, and the Kingdom was advanced. It wasn't about them; it was about Jesus. When people spent time with the disciples, they knew they had been in the presence of Jesus. This is what I longed for, that the works of the Kingdom would come, that the Kingdom would be advanced like it was in the book of Acts.

Sometimes, though, we ask God for something we are not

I never want to have success beyond my character's capacity to sustain it.

prepared to receive, and if God answered us, it would have a detrimental impact on our lives and his Kingdom. I never want to have success beyond my character's capacity to sustain it. Ironically, it is often failures and trials that forge the character necessary for sustainable success.

We must say yes to God in the face of such character-forming, faith-forging trials. This is why I put the *if* in that prayer; I didn't want God to answer a prayer that would surpass the strength of my character and intimacy and disgrace his name. I thank God for redeeming the hardships, trials, tribulations, and failures of my life to forge character within me. I thank God for keeping me from success that my character was not yet ready to sustain. The week I wrote this section of this chapter, I received a "no" to something I had been praying for, an opportunity. And I thanked God for that "no" because I believe He was answering my prayer—*if* my character could sustain it.

The Testing of Time

I want to do something dangerous. I want to talk about my own journey. It is dangerous for two reasons. First, people may confuse what is descriptive for what is prescriptive. This is my journey; I am describing the way God dealt with me. It is descriptive for God's dealings in my life; it is not prescriptive for the way God deals with all people. For sure, there are principles to be gleaned and learned—for example, the principle that testing is an eternal and universal principle. But while there are principles that can be learned, everyone must travel their own path with God, and everyone's story will look different.

Joseph's story involved dreams and interpretations to reveal his destiny, followed by animosity, slavery, and imprisonment to test, refine, and prepare him to fulfill his destiny. David's story involved a prophet coming to reveal and seal David's destiny with a prayer and anointing. David was tested by a terrifying encounter with a real-life giant, and he had to rise above the fear of seasoned warriors to conquer that giant. He was tested through the rantings of a demonized king, and during long seasons in the desert where he was abandoned by many of his friends, chased by his enemies, despised, and isolated. Everyone has a destiny; everyone's character and intimacy with God must be forged through trials and testing—but everyone's destiny and testing are uniquely assigned by God. So I will tell my story as a descriptive process of how God dealt with me.

> Everyone has a destiny; everyone's character and intimacy with God must be forged through trials and testing—but everyone's destiny and testing are uniquely assigned by God.

Second, in telling my story, I risk that you will make the story about me; I don't want you to make the story about me, but about Jesus. This is the testimony of Jesus. Just like the book of Acts is the testimony of Jesus' continued work through the Acts of the Apostles, so this is the testimony of Jesus. I have nothing but empty hands; this was merely the process God took me through to forge my character and intimacy so I could fulfill my destiny for the honor and testimony of Jesus and the advancement of his Kingdom. Please keep that in mind.

Note this. I prayed this prayer—"God, give me the ability to impart your Spirit, *if* my character and intimacy with you can sustain it"—for years with great regularity and consistency, and with hardly any results. Time is always part of the testing process; there is always a delay between the time when the promise of God's call and divine purpose in your life is given, and the time of the fulfillment of that promise.

Time is the ultimate tester of our resolve to hold to the promise and not settle for anything less than God's purpose. Time will reveal our true character and test our passion; time will refine our motives and nearly destroy our dreams. But those who pass the test of time and remain steadfast in trust and relentless pursuit of God and his purposes will be rewarded.

> Time is the ultimate tester of our resolve to hold to the promise and not settle for anything less than God's purpose. Time will reveal our true character and test our passion; time will refine our motives and nearly destroy our dreams.

God often gives us early signs of what is to come. He gives us a taste of what could be, a preview of what will happen if we endure. These early indicators are designed to strengthen us in our time of waiting.

David conquered Goliath, routed the Philistines, and married the king's daughter—all after he was anointed as the next king by Samuel. These were the early signposts of what was later to be fulfilled. But after these early expressions of his divine destiny, David went through a season of trial that was both severe and lasted for a decade.

Early in my ministry, I was praying for a woman at a conference. The instruction from the front was that we were to lay our hands on people, but not pray out loud, and the leaders would pray from the front. Of course, people can't follow instructions, and they put too much emphasis on their own prayers, so people prayed anyway. But I didn't pray out loud; I just laid hands and focused on Jesus as they prayed.

After the session was over, the woman came to me and said, "Did you feel that when you laid your hand on me?" I looked at her with a puzzled expression and asked, "What?" She said, "The heat. Did you feel the heat? Your hand was on fire; I was burning up underneath your hand. I was just hoping you wouldn't move your hand." I didn't feel a thing, but it was the first time in my life that someone had felt heat while I prayed.

God was beginning to answer my prayer; there was an impartation occurring. But I didn't have another experience like that for several more years. I expected the first experience to open the floodgates, but it didn't. This is often how God works. This is part of the testing. God wants to find out if we have the resolve to persevere through the drought of spiritual activity so our character and intimacy can be forged, formed, and finalized in such a way that we can sustain the weight of having the floodgates of the Spirit's activity opened in our life.

I was disappointed that no one else, following that session, felt heat from my hands. This lasted for years. I was even more disappointed when someone else would pray, and the person receiving prayer would feel heat from their hand and not mine. I had to confess that self-focused, proud, sinful stuff to God. The testing of time was critical to purging my self-life to prepare me for receiving more of the Christ-life I longed for. I was disappointed, but I didn't quit asking, seeking, or knocking. Many people allow disappointment to drown out faith rather than allowing disappointment to refine their character so that faith can be developed.

Often when we are disappointed in the slowness of God,

our hearts take offense at God, and we abandon our sacred calling and purpose. This, too, is part of the testing of our faith. We must resolve not to take offense at God, to process all of our disappointments, and to hold steady to what He has promised us. It isn't easy. It requires intestinal fortitude, steely resolve, unrelenting determination, continual processing, death to self, and a steady hand at the wheel.

As time went on, something very important shifted inside of me, and this happened somewhere around forty years old. I started longing for God like never before in my life. Not for what God could do for me or in me or through me, but just for *God Himself*. Not for his benefits, gifts, or fruitfulness—just for Him. Not for happy feelings, or Holy Spirit chills, or manifestations of his presence—just for Him. I started longing for Him more than for success, and I started pursuing Him just for Him.

I wasn't seeking Him so I could see power, but power accompanies his presence—the key to seeing the supernatural is the presence of God. Only God can do the impossible; I had to make the shift from things being too much about me to making it all about Him. It is a hard shift to make, and one that I have to continually revisit. The subtleties of self are so slippery, the pull of self is so strong in our souls—this is why testing is so critical to developing humility and the deep faith that accompanies it. Death to self is an unnatural, unruly, gut-wrenching necessity for deep faith to be formed.

God gave me that dream about revival that I mentioned earlier in December 2006, which I detail in my first book, *Pathways to the King*. The dream was about a coming revival that God was initiating, and my specific assignment in this revival. After a prophetess revealed my role, she said, "Pray for him." And then the lights went out, and I found myself in a dungeon in a fierce battle with a huge demonic beast—a time of severe trial and testing. After the trial was over, I emerged out of the dungeon and another prophetess gave me a sign of the coming revival: as I have explained, the New Orleans Saints would win the Super Bowl. If you are a football fan, you know the Saints went on to win the Super Bowl in February 2010.

When God gave me the dream, I had no idea the trial and testing I was about to enter. But, thankfully, that dream warned me tribulation was coming, and it steadied my resolve to endure the hardship no matter what. I cannot tell you how many times I reviewed that dream as a source of strength in the years that followed. When God gave me the dream, I had no idea the intensity of the trials, nor the length of time it would entail. I was ill prepared to receive the promise—but didn't know this.

I felt God calling me to do two things: First, seek his face. I pursued Him with all my heart for Him alone. It was all about his presence. Second, preach revival until it comes.

I started preaching revival in obedience to Jesus, fully expecting that people would eagerly join me in this pursuit. I'm not sure if that was faith or leadership stupidity, but I was surely in for another big surprise and more disappointment. People were not eagerly joining me on this road. Some revolted, others rebelled, some were divisive, while many others processed out loud (though kindly) with me, and still others thankfully joined me in the pursuit of God and renewal. Sadly, many of those who joined me dropped out along the way, much to my heartache and dismay. They didn't endure the time of testing. The greater the vision, the greater the testing required to see that vision fulfilled. Thankfully, some joined me and have persevered to this day.

During this time, someone actually created a pseudo name on Facebook and started friending everyone in the church and writing against me, calling me a heretic. They ended up contacting the District Office in an attempt to have me fired

over my "heretical" views, which fortunately were in alignment with the doctrines of my denomination, so nothing
came of the effort. God actually gave me a prophetic prompting to call the district to warn them that this person was going
to call and attack me; I called the office the very day the person contacted them with accusations against me. Only God.
Other people blogged against me; I actually had radio shows
air against me in the area. And then there were all the people who just murmured and complained and left the church.
It was a gut-wrenching season. I continually sought the Lord
and asked, "Am I doing the right thing? I'm just trying to do
what you told me. Am I doing the right thing?" And all the
Lord said to me was, "Keep your hand to the plow, and don't
look back." So I plowed ahead with weak and faltering faith.

In the midst of that terrible season of deep pain, I went to
the monastery to meet with God. I cried out to Him: "I don't
understand. I just don't get it. Why are people so upset? Why
am I getting killed? I am just doing what you asked me to do;
I am just preaching on revival. Why?"

And much to my surprise, again, the Lord answered me
in a most unexpected way: "I am answering your prayers."
Honestly, I had no idea what He was talking about, so I said,
"Lord, if you tell me what I'm praying, I promise, I'll stop." I
heard the Spirit clearly say, "You have prayed for over a decade, 'Give me the ability to impart your Spirit, if my character
and intimacy can sustain it.' I am answering your prayer. This
is what it takes."

I laid facedown on the floor and said through pain-
streaked tears: "Lord, answer my prayer. No matter what.
Answer my prayer." I embraced the trials, testing, and time
delays necessary to form my character and intimacy enough
to sustain God's purpose for my life. But, please understand,
while I sought to surrender to God's work in me, that doesn't
mean I didn't doubt. I struggled with doubt nearly every day.

I thought, *Am I doing the right thing? Is God really going to answer my prayer? Is this ever going to pay off?* Every day I had to summon the courage to stay the course and believe God could redeem this.

After years of attack came years of unanswered prayer. I have prayed for four promises God made to me, including this one about revival, for more than a decade. For most of that time, I saw a little forward movement on these promises, but not much. After the Saints won the Super Bowl in 2010, I fervently and expectantly prayed and anticipated a fresh spiritual outpouring that would usher in another great awakening. But things went along at SSCC and in the other places that I minister much like they had before. There was no dramatic increase, no significant change, no evidential outpouring of the Spirit. More time, more trials, more testing, more purging, more forming of my character and intimacy, more forging of my faith.

There were small signs of forward progress, but not what I expected. There were, for example, new numbers of people seeking God with fervor. There were more leaders open to the things of God than ever before in my circles of influence. I was grateful for these things, but they weren't what I was hoping or longing for—instead, they were distant clouds on the horizon.

The truth is that it didn't feel like all this was forging faith in me. Actually, at times I felt like I was losing hope; it felt like I was slipping backward on the spectrum of faith. But despite all my doubts and questions, I kept my hand to the plow as the Lord had told me. Sometimes faith looks like nothing more than a weak, wobbly, perseverance.

One of the promises God had given us as a church was about a large piece of land we had purchased. We purchased the land because we anticipated a coming revival, and because we had been growing as a church. But now the growth stopped, and people started leaving—yet we had this huge piece of land

and a big debt to go with it. And as people departed, our finances took a hit, and we had less financial means to support the bigger financial obligation. We had prayed and fasted over this purchase and sensed, as a leadership team, that God was calling us to this faith venture. But no miraculous answers came forth, and there was no supernatural deliverance. Finally, much to my heartache and consternation we had to sell the land.

> The trials that test our faith sometimes feel as though they are snuffing out the final flickering candle flame. But always remember this about Jesus: "A bruised reed he will not break, and a smoldering wick he will not snuff out" (Isaiah 42:3).

I got to a place where I was so disappointed with all these unfulfilled promises and unanswered prayers that I wrestled with a question I had never wrestled with before: *Does God lie?* I talk about that in detail in *River Dwellers*. I knew I couldn't stay in ministry if I couldn't grope my way through the darkness of that question.

The trials that test our faith sometimes feel as though they are snuffing out the final flickering candle flame. But always remember this about Jesus: "A bruised reed he will not break, and a smoldering wick he will not snuff out" (Isaiah 42:3). He doesn't test us to snuff out the smoldering wick of our faith; he tests us to turn that spark into a fire. He is the master teacher, and you can resolve to hold on to what He has promised because He is good.

Eventually, I got through that trying question of whether God lies with a revelation, from Hebrews 11, that God sometimes fulfills his promise in the next generation. There are times we need to view our promises in light of eternity. We are but one link in an eternal Kingdom, and we need to be willing to fight for the promises of God for the next generation, for the sake of God's eternal plan and purposes. We make it too much about us and too little about God; it is like an electric short in the power cord of our faith. The problem is perspective. Sometimes we are at the front end of the link in the chain, and we think the promise is for us and we fight for it to be fulfilled in our generation – as we should. But, we do not understand or see that we are the first link in the chain, and that God has raised up others after us to see fulfilled what we were only called to see and fight for.

God asked me: *Will you fight for revival if you never see it, so the next generation can usher it in?* It wasn't what I wanted, but I surrendered, gave God my unconditional yes to that question, and fought on with newfound faith. I was willing to never see revival, but fight for the next generation to live out the promise God had given me. However, I knew God wasn't necessarily saying I *wouldn't* see revival, He was just asking me if I was willing—He was testing my faith. I surrendered to God's call, and my soul was at peace, but the testing still wasn't over. Trials always lead us to the place of surrender. Surrender is critical to the cultivation of humility, and humility is essential for the development of faith.

The next season of my life was the dark night of the soul. Amid all this, the lights went out, and God disappeared on me. People often speak of "the dark night of the soul" as if it were about hardship, but St. John of the Cross wasn't talking about hardship when he coined the term. He was talking about the absence of the presence of God; our senses become dulled to the presence of God, by God's doing.

Again, God in his mercy gave me a preview of this season of life before it came. I had read St. John's book on the Dark Night, and I had read Thomas Ashbrook's book, *Mansions of the Heart,* both of which prepared me for this season of spiritual darkness.

One day I was at the monastery. It was in a season of my life in which I was hearing God's voice and experiencing God's presence like never before. It was as if I was living in a flood-plain of revelation. During this season, I read about the dark night of the soul, and I went out for a walk and wept. I said, "Lord, I love your presence; I love your voice. I don't want to go through the dark night of the soul." As I was talking to the Lord about the dark night, He said to me: *Even though you cannot sense me, I will still be there with you, and if you look for me, you can find me.* That prepared me for the trial that was to come.

It was during this battle with disappointment, and wrestling with the question of whether God lies, that the lights went out. I couldn't think of a worse time for this. I went through *months* where I could not sense God anymore, nor hear his voice. It was dark, quiet, silent, empty, and lonely. Every day I came to sit with God, most days in silence, waiting through tears. And every day there was nothing but empty silence. My faith in all the promises of God felt like it was at an all-time low, as though nothing but a smoldering wick. But the master teacher had not set out to fail me in this test, nor to destroy my faith, but to ensure that I could ace the test and develop my faith. He would not let the smoldering wick go out so long as I kept looking to Him, so long as I refused to quit. I was more convinced of my nothingness, and my emptiness, than ever before. It was just where He needed me to be.

Finally, one day alone with God, his presence returned. It still moves me to tears to think about the return of his presence, because I had missed Him so much. I knew, from reading *The Dark Night of the Soul,* that the purpose of the dark night was purgation. God was purging, purifying me. This was the testing of faith that James spoke of, where our character is formed.

I didn't always know how He was forming my character, and when I asked Him for wisdom in this season, I didn't get any answers, because He was silent. What amazed me most as I emerged from that season is that my faith was strengthened; I came out of the dark night of the soul with a deeper, stronger faith than ever before. In this season of darkness, my faith felt weaker than it ever had, and yet somehow coming out of that season my faith was like a flower emerging in springtime. It sprung into bloom! From the depths of the darkness of the earth the seed grows, and suddenly the flower emerges, springs forth . . . and blooms.

Tools for Trials

When the trials came with all their ferocity, I felt like I was not at all prepared to live through them, but God gave me tools to get through. God gives us what we need to emerge through a season of testing victoriously—just like a good teacher who teaches you what you need to know to ace the test. He teaches you what you need to know before the test. We have to review our past for the tools God has given us so we can utilize them in our present to get to our future.

God gave Joseph a couple of dreams and his ever-present favor that promoted him through every hole he found himself in. God gave David victories over the bear, the lion, and the giant, and a prophetic word about his future destiny from a reliable prophet who was a proven source of God's clear direction. They both had to hang tightly to the tools God had given them in the light when the darkness came upon them. God had given me a dream with a sign, prophetic words, some critically important encounters and whispers, and some formative lessons about intimacy that saw me through. Look to your past to gain the keys to your present that can open the doors to your future. And walk through the hallways to your destiny, recognizing that sometimes those hallways feel like a confusing labyrinth that take quite a bit of time to get through.

Know this: If you persist, if you hold tightly to what God has told you, if you keep doing the right things, if you demonstrate steely resolve to hold on to what God has for you for as long as it takes, if you take an eternal perspective, you will find your way through the testing, and your faith will be developed from hope . . . to expectation . . . and even to certainty.

God told me to keep my hand to the plow and not look back. Over and over again I repeated that phrase to myself through the darkest valleys, trusting that eventually He would lead me out of the dark and into the light once again. This is why we can consider it pure joy when the trials come. "Because you know that the testing of your faith produces perseverance. Let perseverance finish its work so that you may be mature and complete, not lacking anything" (James 1:3, 4). Imagine a faith that is so certain that it lacks nothing. Wow! It can't happen without the trials and testing of our faith. It's hard, but it's worth it. Persevere. Keep your hand to the plow.

When I first started doing Holy Spirit weekends and praying for people to be filled with the Spirit, I would see someone get filled with the Spirit visibly and demonstrably once in a while. But after emerging from this season of testing, after my faith was forged by God in the darkness, there was a dramatic shift. The first conference I spoke at after this season, I laid hands on people in prayer and they started experiencing the power and presence of God in new ways and with new regularity. It was right after I came through the dark night of the soul that I noticed this new spiritual power.

When I prayed for people at that conference, I saw more of the supernatural activity of God than I ever had. Something was shifting. I prayed for several people who were leaders of important Kingdom ventures, and God came upon them in power. The Spirit was manifest, and several of them fell over under the weight of God's presence, something that had never happened to any of them before. They fell to the ground like the apostle John in Revelation 1 as they experienced the heavy presence of God. Some people were filled with joy and laughed; some people cried under the weighty presence of the tender, loving affections of the Father.

I was preaching messages on the baptism or fullness of the Spirit to audiences that were not used to manifestations of the Holy Spirit, and when we prayed, the same manifestations would come. I have nothing, just empty hands. It was simply the presence of God. I had seen these sorts of things before, but not like this, not to this degree. And it was only the beginning of this new season.

The manifest presence of God has been increasing ever since. It has been humbling and amazing to watch. The last conference I did, at the time of this writing, I experienced something I've never seen before. I preached on the baptism of the Spirit and asked anyone who wanted to be filled with the Spirit to stand. I've given this talk, or a close version of it, in a half-dozen places, and every time the vast majority of people stand up. This time, probably ninety percent of the crowd stood, and I simply prayed, "Come, Holy Spirit." People started falling over. People fell over who didn't know that was normal when the supernatural visits the natural. People fell over in a church where no one had fallen over in a hundred years. People fell over before anyone laid hands on them. God came and imparted his Spirit in answer to a twenty-year-old prayer and a decade of testing that had hit its mark.

The master teacher once again had helped a faltering, stumbling, struggling student to ace a test. The master teacher once again had formed the heart and soul through his inner work so He could release the outer works of the Kingdom through a prepared and readied vessel who had nothing but empty hands.

Reflection Questions

1. What has God used to develop humility in your life?

2. What does authentic humility look like? What did it look like in Paul's life? What does it look like in your life?

3. Where is God attempting to develop humility in you at this time? How are you cooperating with Him or resisting?

4. How has testing played a role in your spiritual development, the formation of humility, and the strengthening of your faith? What key lessons have you learned through testing?

5. What tests are you enduring? What is God trying to teach you? How is He trying to shape you? How can you cooperate with his developmental efforts? What tools has God given you to prepare you to pass this test? Do you fundamentally trust the master teacher to redeem this test in your life?

Six:
The Holy Spirit and Faith

"Very truly I tell you, it is for your good that I am going away. Unless I go away, the Advocate will not come to you."

—JESUS (JOHN 16:7)

When Jesus departed from his disciples, He did not leave them alone, but He sent them the Holy Spirit, the comforter, the counselor, the advocate, the Spirit of truth to be with them. The Holy Spirit guides us through the treacherous parts of our spiritual pilgrimage. He comes alongside us when discouragement threatens to snuff out the candle of our faith; He nurtures the flame to keep it burning. He is with us in the valley of testing; it was the Spirit who made known to us the tools we would need to make it through this valley, and it is He who comes along now and reminds us that we were given these tools before we even got to this dark valley. He is nearer still to us when the lights go out in the dark night of the soul, though we cannot sense Him. Yet if we can learn to spot the signs of his presence, we will see the evidence that He is in fact with us, strengthening us to make it through, gently guiding us as we grope in the dark, helping us to trust in the darkness and leading us back to the light again.

In this chapter I want to examine three key roles the Holy Spirit plays in helping develop our faith. We could talk about many other things, but these are the three I feel most compelled to write about.

I could not have made it through the seasons of testing that I described in the previous chapter without the presence and help of the Holy Spirit. I suspect when we get to Heaven we will finally see all things for what they really are; only then will we see how we made it through some of our most difficult deserts in life because someone was praying for us even though we didn't know it. Only in Heaven will we understand the contribution that others' words, prayers, and support made to our formation and development. We will have a list of people we owe a debt of gratitude to, but at the very top of the list will be the Holy Spirit. He has been a frequently unseen source of strength, help, courage, and comfort to your life and mine. I am grateful for all He has done behind the scenes that I am not even aware of in my life. I want to develop a closeness to Him, a sensitivity to his working, so that I am more readily cooperating with all his supportive activity.

The Spirit Reveals the Father's Love

The Holy Spirit strengthens our faith by revealing the love of the Father to us; the more we are secure in God's love, the more we trust Him. Romans 5:5 says, "God's love has been poured out into our hearts through the Holy Spirit, who has been given to us." Paul goes on to explain, in Romans 8:15-17: "The Spirit you received does not make you slaves, so that you live in fear again; rather, the Spirit you received brought about your adoption to sonship. And by him we cry, 'Abba, Father.' The Spirit himself testifies with our spirit that we are God's children. Now if we are children, then we are heirs—heirs of God and co-heirs with Christ, if indeed we share in his sufferings in order that we may also share in his glory."

The Holy Spirit reveals the adoptive love of the Father to us so that we will know we are children of God. If we know that we are children, we will not pray in fear, act in fear, or live in fear. If, through the revelation of the Spirit, we know that we are children of God, then we will pray like members of the family coming to a kind and good Father, delighted to enter his presence, eager to receive his gracious response. We won't timidly ask, trying to overcome his reluctance or being fearful of untimely explosions at our annoying requests. We won't avoid asking because we are concerned that we could possibly be a nuisance, bothering a busy Father consumed with more important things than our petitions, or a preoccupied Father attending to people more important than us. Shame will not keep us at a distance; the perfect love of the Father revealed by the Spirit will give us confidence to approach, knowing our sins are covered, and we are welcome to the throne.

> The more we are convinced, through the revelation of the Spirit, of the Father's love, the more we will ask with confidence and even certainty.

The more we are convinced, through the revelation of the Spirit, of the Father's love, the more we will ask with confidence and even certainty. Love bids us come, gives us confidence, beckons us to the throne, calls us his own. Why, then, are so many praying with such weak faith? Is it possible that we know about the Father's love, but do not *know* the Father's love firsthand through the revelatory, experiential knowledge of the Spirit? Sometimes we can give all the right answers about the Father's love on a theology test, yet we still do not live in the reality of that which we can articulate. When it comes to truth, articulation without revelation leads to deprivation.

The Spirit of God is good at what He does, and according to Paul, He reveals the Father's love and testifies with our spirits that we are children of God. Yet many do not pray out of the confident assurance of adoptive love. It isn't because the Spirit has failed his work, but often we have blocks that keep us from receiving the revelation of the adoptive love of the Father. Most of these blocks are soul blocks, and the Spirit not only knows what they are, He also knows how to remove them. We must go to Him for help in removing the blocks, and we must go to Him for revelation of the Father's adoptive love if we are going to ask confidently like children and not beg cowardly like fearful outsiders to the family, or even as slaves, as Paul says. This is why I wrote the book *Soul Care,* because many people, including myself, have been helped on their spiritual journey through the principles in that book. Often we need help removing these blocks. Books, wise guides, counselors, and conferences can help us discover and remove some of the blocks that prevent us from receiving revelation of the Father's love.

One day it occurred to me that the member of the Trinity that I least connected with was the Father. I loved Jesus; I couldn't read enough about Him in the Gospels. My first supernatural encounter with God was a picture of Jesus, and his love was revealed to me in that moment. It changed me forever. And I loved and connected to the Holy Spirit because I could feel his presence and hear his voice.

But the Father felt distant to me, and I felt avoidance in my soul toward the Father, a reluctance to come to Him. I *knew* the Father loved me, because the Bible told me so, but I didn't *feel* loved by the Father; I even felt a little fearful in his presence. I didn't even call Him "Father"; I called Him "God" when I addressed Him in prayer. It wasn't a conscious choice; it was merely a symptomatic expression of a deeper issue, but it was the clue that made me begin to see I had an issue that needed to be addressed.

There was some sort of block between me and the Father, and that block was hindering the work of the Spirit to pour out and reveal the adoptive love of the Father in my heart. I didn't know what the block was, but I knew God knew, so I sought Him. I asked Him to remove the block and reveal the Father to me.

I spoke to Jesus one day about it. "Jesus, I don't know the Father like you know the Father," I prayed. "Show me the Father like you see Him." I kept praying that prayer over the next few months. What I was hoping was to get closer to the Father, to remove the block that hindered my intimacy with Him, to overcome the avoidance I felt in my soul toward Him. And thankfully, all of that happened. But what I didn't expect was how the revelation of the Father's adoptive love would change the strength of my trust in God.

A woman called me from church one day and asked if she could take me on a prayer journey. She said she felt like this was something God had shown her. It was a way to pray with people, and she wanted me to experience it so I could give it my blessing and she could practice this prayer with others. She was a lovely older woman in my church who was an intercessor, and I love intercessors, but they can be a little weird sometimes. If you are an intercessor, I assure you that I mean no offense when I say that, and I covet your prayers and value your input! But let's be honest: sometimes it gets a little odd! I reluctantly went on this prayer journey. I brought one of my staff members with me . . . just in case. She was a little nervous too, and on our drive over she told me she was glad I was going through this experience rather than her.

When we got there, this sweet woman served us a cup of

tea and then explained what she wanted to do. She wanted to allow the Holy Spirit to direct the prayer time with pictures. Now, I believe the Holy Spirit speaks in pictures—in dreams and visions. I've read the Bible, and there are plenty of those kinds of encounters with God in Scripture, and I've had some of those in my own life. But that isn't the typical way I hear from God. My wife is a seer; most of what she receives from the Spirit comes in the form of pictures. But that's not true of me. Nonetheless, I was there, and I was willing to go along with it.

She asked me to picture a peaceful place, a peaceful image in my mind. So I closed my eyes, and the image that came to mind was of a waterfall in the woods. It was lovely and very peaceful. Then she simply asked Jesus to come into the picture and lead me where He wanted to take me.

With that, I had an image of Jesus come to me at the waterfall and take me by the hand; He led me upward to Heaven. We were walking on the clouds, and out in the distance I saw a castle. Jesus was huge, and although I was full-grown in the picture, compared to the size of Him, I looked like a toddler. He was holding my hand as we walked along the clouds, and He said to me, "I am taking you to see the Father."

Deb, my staff member, told me on our way home that, at this point, she wondered if this meant I was going to die. I'm happy to report, however, that I'm still here (at least at the time of this writing)!

The scene changed, and now I saw myself as a toddler, and Jesus was throwing me in the air and catching me. He was laughing, and so was I. It was a scene I was very familiar with, because I had done this with all my children when they were little. We never did arrive at the castle, though that is what I expected would happen when I first saw it in the distance.

The whole prayer experience was extremely peaceful. The woman was very loving and gentle, and I sensed the Spirit the whole time. But it wasn't until I went home and journaled about it, and processed the experience, that I finally figured out what the Spirit was doing. *He was showing me the Father.*

Jesus said He was going to show me the Father, and when He was throwing me in the air and delighting in me, that was the face of the Father, that was how the Father felt about me. When this revelation of the Spirit came to me at home, I wept; it was the first time I had felt the Father's delight over me. I had delighted in my children as a father, but I had never felt the delight of the Father in me as his child.

It is one thing to know you are loved by God, but it is a holy, other thing to have the adoptive love of the Father revealed to your heart by the Spirit. There is a life altering gap between knowledge and revelation. When the truth of the Father's adoptive love shifts from your head to your heart, you are bound to trust Him more. The people who love us most are the people we open up to the deepest, because we trust them. Love is the cornerstone of trust. But love that is cognitively understood without being experienced doesn't fuel deep trust. When there are blocks in our soul that prevent us from receiving the fullness of the Father's love, there will be suspicion in our life that questions the Father's goodness, and our faith will be weakened. We need the revelation of the adoptive love of the Father, and this is what the Spirit does within us.

I had another encounter with the Father's love that changed everything for me. I speak of it elsewhere, but it bears repeating here because of its direct link to faith. At the time of this prayer journey, and the time I had this next encounter with the love of the Father, I was in the middle of the time of testing. Even after I had this first encounter with the revelation of the Father's love, I still prayed for more, because I knew the block had not been completely lifted. I made progress, but there was more ground to make up, so I persisted with my prayer for Jesus to show me the Father.

One night I had a dream that revolutionized my relationship with the Father. In the dream I was finishing up a weekend of speaking at a men's retreat. There were a couple hundred men in the room, and as I was making my way out of the building, all the men came up to me to hug me and say goodbye. They gave me the typical man hug . . . three hard pats on the back and then you're done. Anything more than that is definitely suspicious in most men's worlds! So I walked toward the exit, and all these guys kept hugging me and patting me solidly on the back. Finally, I got to the door and met someone who had once been very critical of me. But in the dream he was friendly, and I walked past him to the parking lot.

There was one last man in the lot. He was an older man, old enough to be my father, and when I got to him he hugged me. Everyone else hugged me, so that was not surprising, but what was surprising was that no one had taught this man the man hug rules! He held me and held me and wouldn't let go. The whole time he held me in this awkward embrace, I could feel my skin crawling. Finally, he broke the hug, but still he didn't completely let me go. Instead, he took me by both of my shoulders and looked me in the eyes and said, "I am your Father in Heaven, and I love you." I lost it. I woke up sobbing; my pillow was soaking wet. In the dream I collapsed into his arms and he just hugged me, but I no longer tried to get away.

That dream completely changed the way I interacted with the Father. Before that, the Father felt distant, aloof, even a little scary. But ever since that dream, the thing I most feel from the Father is his tender affections.

Dreams are symbolic, and symbols have meaning. I was speaking at a men's retreat because I had an identity wound that God needed to address. I am a man, so my identity is directly connected to my masculinity. My masculinity wound had left me with a shame that made me reluctant to approach the Father and left me feeling avoidant. Shame is a powerful emotion that leaves us distant in our relationships from both God and others. It must be removed if we are going to experience the adoptive love of the Father. My shame left me feeling like I didn't have what it takes, like I was unworthy or unlovable. These things weren't conscious thoughts, but they were the deep issues of the heart that had left me distant from the Father.

The man who was critical of me represented the critic within me; often we are our own worst critics, and I was battling with internal shame that could only be cured by revelation of the Father's love. Often the hardest person to get past is the critic within, and until I got past that gatekeeper of my soul, I could not experience the Father's love and trust Him with new levels of certainty. Often our self-talk reveals

> Often our self-talk reveals that we have a critic within. What goes unfiltered through our minds reveals what is undealt with in our souls.

that we have a critic within. What goes unfiltered through our minds reveals what is undealt with in our souls. We must pay attention to the self-talk that reveals our inner critic, and we must break the inner critic's grip on our soul if we are going to experience the Father's love.

Moses had this same deep shame, a toxic shame that kept him from drawing near the Father when the Father first revealed Himself to Moses. Actually, Moses' initial reaction to the revelation of God was to hide his face from God. We hide our face when we are wrestling with shame. And his initial question to the calling of God was, "Who am I?" He was struggling with a shame-based identity issue, and so was I. Both Moses and I needed the revelation of the Father's tender love to cure that wound and remove that shame block.

The discomfort I felt in that very lengthy hug from the Father was once again my shame at play, one that left me with an intimacy barrier. Getting too close made my skin crawl; it is indicative of a fear that we will be found wanting and ultimately not acceptable. It is a fear that if people really knew us, they wouldn't really love us. It is hard to receive love when we perceive ourselves at some level as unlovable. Toxic shame leaves us with a Teflon soul: love doesn't stick, it just slides off.

The Spirit knew the barriers that were keeping me from the love of the Father, He revealed them to me in a dream, and He removed them in an outpouring of the Father's love. It was a game-changer for me in my intimacy with the Father. But it also changed the depth of my trust with God.

After that theophany, in which the Father appeared to me in the dream, I prayed with more confidence. I prayed with more certainty. I approached the throne with more boldness, confidence, peace, and acceptance. I approached as a child who knew his Father delighted in him.

It was only after that encounter that I would pray for people with great regularity that the Father's love would be poured out in their hearts, which is clearly God's will (1 John 5:14, 15; Romans 5:5), and people would start weeping as the revelation of the Father's love was poured out to them. Jesus told his disciples, "Freely you have received; freely give." We can't give what we don't have. Once we have received the Father's tender affections, we can begin to give it away in prayer to others.

Sometimes I would get a feeling of deep compassion for someone, and I knew beyond any doubt it wasn't Jesus' compassion or the Spirit's compassion; this was clearly the tenderness of the Father. I would go up to them and say, "I feel the Father's compassion for you," and they would begin to weep. It was uncanny; it happened dozens of times, and it happened to me again just this week. I saw a woman walk into a room, and as soon as I saw her, I could feel the compassion of the Father. I knew she was carrying sadness in her soul, though I didn't know why. I went up to her and said, "When I saw you today, I could feel the Father's compassion for you, and it seems to me that you are carrying some sadness in your soul." She started crying, told me the cause of her sadness, and I hugged her and prayed with her.

I was no longer a slave captive to fear, with shame deep inside my soul; I was certain of my sonship at a whole new level of depth within my soul because of the revelation of the Spirit. The Spirit had testified with my spirit that He was my Father in Heaven who loved me (Romans 8:16). "Now if we are children, then we are heirs—heirs of God and co-heirs of Christ, if indeed we share in his sufferings in order that we may also share in his glory" (Romans 8:17). I had shared in some of his sufferings. He had revealed the Father's love to me, and now I was praying like an heir of God, a co-heir with Christ.

Here is the thing: for many years, I didn't know I had a block with the Father. The hard part about self-awareness is that our experiences are normative for us, so we don't realize when they are below the norms of God. We read these things in Scripture and they are familiar to us, and we have heard them and read them before, so we think, Yes. I know that. I know the Father loves me. But we confuse our intellectual knowledge with actual revelatory experience. If you had asked me in my twenties if I knew the Father loved me, I would have said yes. If you had asked me if I had experienced the Father's love, I would have said yes. I thought I had, and to some degree I had, but there was a block I was not aware of, and it was limiting my experience and my faith.

Perhaps the most remarkable aftereffect of this revelation of the Father's love is that we approach God as an heir, a co-heir with Christ. The things that belong to Jesus belong to us; we now have access to these things. This is theologically accurate, but we will never pray with that sort of confidence unless we know the love of the Father through the revelation of the Spirit in ever-increasing measure. As our identity is sealed through the Spirit as an heir of God, we pray with new levels of active trust and certain faith, and we see the works of the Kingdom more readily manifest.

Though we still come with nothing but empty hands, we come with confidence to a Father who delights in his children and has unlimited resources. Though we approach the throne of God with all our weakness, we come as an heir to the throne of One who has infinite strength.

The Spirit Speaks

If we are going to develop our faith, we need to hear the Holy Spirit's voice. I could not have made it through the long season of testing in my life without the Holy Spirit's guidance, wisdom, and revelation. There were bends in the road I could not have navigated, narrow passageways I could not have traversed, cliffs I could not have scaled, and dark thickets I could not have seen my way through without the Spirit to guide me. I wrote a chapter on how to hear God's voice in *River Dwellers*. If you have never learned how to hear God speak personally to you, or if you don't hear God's voice regularly, I encourage you to pick up that book and learn how to become sensitive to the Spirit's promptings. But, for this chapter, let's look at how the whispers of the Spirit help us develop faith.

The Spirit gives us guidance. There were times during the season of testing that I didn't know what to do, and I felt helpless and weak, but I would wait on God, and He would give me a key piece of wisdom I needed.

Sometimes He gave me the wisdom to know what He was doing in me—like when I was on the monastery floor and He said to me, "I'm answering your prayer." That morsel of wisdom from the Spirit gave me enduring courage to stay the course through the worst of the testing, because I knew God was up to something critically important in me. It strengthened my resolve to cooperate with God and surrender to the work of God in my soul.

James 1 tells us that we can rejoice in trials and tribulations because God can redeem these tests in our lives to perfect us, and if we don't know how He can redeem them or what He is trying to do in us, we can ask Him for wisdom. Many times during that long season of testing, and during my entire lifetime, I have claimed this promise and sought God until He revealed to me how He was trying to form Christ in me. And many times He answered, and it gave me courage, wisdom, or comfort in my time of need. Even in the dark night of the soul when I couldn't hear the Spirit's voice, I felt his inner reassurance that He would redeem this dark night in my life to purge me.

> When you are in the thickets of trial, stop and seek Him. Pray and wait on Him for wisdom; don't give up asking and seeking for his guidance until it comes.

The voice of the Spirit in those situations most often did not take away my trial; it merely gave me what I needed to navigate that leg of the journey safely and with the Father's purposeful perspective. I couldn't have made it through without Him guiding me. When you are in the thickets of trial, stop and seek Him. Pray and wait on Him for wisdom; don't give up asking and seeking for his guidance until it comes.

I was deeply discouraged one day because someone had publicly attacked me on a prominent website. The person attacked one of my books, though I have sincerely and painstakingly written each of them to honor Jesus and help people who want to follow Him. I was processing the grief of public humiliation with the Comforter when I heard Him speak a word of wisdom that has helped me countless times since. He brought my attention to Matthew 5:11, 12: "Blessed are you when people insult you, persecute you and falsely say all kinds of evil against you because of me. Rejoice and be glad, because great is your reward in heaven, for in the same way they persecuted the prophets who were before you."

It was like reading the passage for the first time. I can rejoice and be glad in persecution because "great is my reward in heaven." I heard the Spirit say, "You owe this guy a debt of gratitude; he is increasing your reward in heaven." I had never thought about personal attacks in that way, and then I heard Him say, "He has elevated you to the status of the prophets (for in the same way they persecuted the prophets who were before you)." Wow! I never viewed attacks the same way. This man was attacking me for that which Jesus had commissioned me, and as a result the Holy Spirit assured me He would recompense me. That revelation broke the weightiness of the attacks I was under, and I felt joy. It changed my perspective, and for the first time in my life, I was truly and freely able to rejoice in persecution and attacks. This is often what the Spirit does: He enlightens us with a revelation that helps us see life from Heaven's perspective and thus unburdens our soul.

> This is often what the Spirit does: He enlightens us with a revelation that helps us see life from Heaven's perspective and thus unburdens our soul.

When many people started speaking against me, the Spirit gave me another invaluable word of wisdom. One day He said to me, "These people are not your enemy. You have an enemy; they are influenced by the enemy of your soul, but they are not your enemy." He led me to bless them, to pray against the spiritual forces of evil that were behind their actions.

Paul conveyed this same truth to the Ephesians: "For our struggle is not against flesh and blood, but against the rulers, against the authorities, against the powers of this dark world and against the spiritual forces of evil in the heavenly realms" (Ephesians 6:12). During this season of my life, when I was subjected to many attacks and was the target of many critical words, the Spirit brought this phrase to my mind, over and over again: "These people are not your enemy." I continued to pray blessings on them, and forgive them, and the Spirit's guidance allowed me to survive that trial without becoming bitter.

Another time the Spirit gave me a dream revealing a group of people who would leave our church. He showed me who the leader of this divisive action would be, and even their motive for what they would do. He revealed this to me before it happened, so that when it did take place I was neither surprised nor dismayed. Everything, even the motives, were eventually revealed just as He had shown me. I was strengthened to endure through the prior knowledge given by revelation of the Spirit. Hardship has a way of clouding our lenses of reality and loosening our grip on Heaven's perspective. The Spirit gives us guidance to cleanse our lens of reality and strengthen our grip on Heaven's perspective. He strengthens our faith with his words.

No matter what may come into our life, Jesus isn't nervous. Jesus told us that "When he, the Spirit of truth, comes, he will guide you into all the truth. He will not speak on his own; he will speak only what he hears, and he will tell you what is yet to come" (John 16:13). Jesus told us that the Spirit could guide us into truth and tell us things that were yet to come. The Sprit revealed the dream to me that revival was coming, and gave me a sign of something yet to come—the Saints would win the Super Bowl—so I would be strengthened in my time of testing, encouraged in time of fear, and fortified in the beastly attacks of the enemy. I wouldn't have made it through with the promise intact in my heart without the preemptive guidance of the Spirit.

The Spirit's guidance not only helped me through the difficult places with wisdom about what He was doing in my soul, but also with knowledge of what was to come and what would result from the time of testing. When these things came to pass just as He showed me, my trust in Him was immensely fortified.

When the Spirit delivers on what He says, we learn to trust Him more. When He delivers repeatedly through times of testing and trial, we learn to trust Him implicitly. Listening to the Spirit's voice, obeying what He says, and watching Him come through—all of this deepens our faith. We must carve out regular times to listen to the Spirit. We have to create an inner stillness so we can increase our sensitivity to his voice. We must increase our times of silence and listening when we are in seasons of testing. We need the voice of God to deepen the development of our faith.

The Spirit Strengthens Us

One of my favorite prayers in the Bible is Paul's intercession for the church at Ephesus, in chapter 3. Paul writes, "I pray that out of his glorious riches he may strengthen you with power through his Spirit in your inner being, so that Christ may dwell in your hearts through faith" (3:16, 17). Paul prays the Spirit would strengthen them with power in their inner being so that two things can happen. First, so Christ may dwell in their hearts through faith. Of course, they are believers, so Christ already dwells in their hearts through faith, but Paul is praying for an increase: *more* of Jesus' presence and fullness in their lives. But in order for them to have the capacity for an increase of the presence of Jesus, they need to have thicker walls in their souls. Their inner being must be strengthened by the Spirit's power. We have as much of the Spirit as we can handle, and the only way we can bear the weight of more of his presence is to have greater capacity or thicker interior walls of the soul.

The other thing Paul asks is that by these thicker walls and increased capacity, through the Spirit's inner strengthening, they may experience the fullness of God's love. Ephesians 3:17f, "And I pray that you, being rooted and established in love, may have power, together with all the Lord's holy people, to grasp how wide and long and high and deep is the love of Christ, and to know this love that surpasses knowledge – that you may be filled to the measure of all the fullness of God." For more of Jesus, and more of his love, they need greater capacity; they need to draw from the strength of the Spirit.

This is true for us as well in our times of hardship and testing. We must draw from the strength of the Spirit. It is often through hardship that the walls of a person's soul grow thicker, and it is often in hardship that we are moved to draw upon the Spirit's strength. The Spirit can strengthen us to overcome; the Spirit can strengthen us to have greater capacity for more of God's presence in our lives. The Spirit can strengthen us to receive more of the adoptive love of the Father—and in all of these things, as this work is accomplished, our faith will increase, so we must learn to draw upon the Spirit's strength in our lives.

Jesus called the Holy Spirit a Comforter or Counselor. He is the one who comes alongside and helps. He is a healer. I can't tell you how many times in my life the Holy Spirit has brought me comfort. I have felt his presence in my loneliness, and I have heard Him whisper, "I am with you." I have received his strength in my weakness, consoling me and encouraging me to fight on because the victory was certain. I have experienced his acceptance in times of rejection, telling me that his love was enough for me. I have sensed his peace overshadow my angst as He imparted the atmosphere of Heaven into my soul. Heaven is a superior realm to Earth because Heaven is eternal. When we learn to tap into the Spirit's strength, Heaven's peace triumphs over Earth's anxieties.

In the early days of our marriage, my wife Jen didn't like me for a season. The Spirit revealed the depths of his love to me and began to heal my broken heart and restore my broken soul. In the season when people spoke ill of me and left the church, the Spirit steadied my nerves, healed my wounds, overcame my rejection with his acceptance, and fortified me with courage to the stay the course He had me on. He told me ahead of time the trial that was coming, and was present with me as a Comforter through it, constantly guiding me through to get to the future destiny He had planned for me.

Don't get me wrong. I am not saying I was an innocent victim in these situations. I wasn't; my sin and brokenness contributed to many of these problems. But God comes and comforts us, and strengthens us, even though we are part of the problem. He redeems these hardships and forms Christ in us. He comforts us and corrects us; He strengthens us and develops us. He sees our part, and sees what is done, and He loves us through it all. He is enough for us no matter what happens. And when we are strengthened, comforted, and developed through the Spirit's activity in these difficult times, we discover that we can trust Him. His grip on us strengthens our grip on Him, and our faith is formed.

Many times I sat with the Spirit in my pain, and I wouldn't even speak. I was past words. I had journaled all I could journal and processed all I could process. All I needed was Him and his healing presence. So I would come and sit in silence.

Psalm 62:1: "For God alone my soul waits in silence, from Him comes my salvation" (ESV). I often sat with that verse in my heart and with my empty hands, and I waited. I waited on the Comforter to do what only He could do for me: heal, comfort, renew, and transform.

There were long seasons when I would come every day and just sit in silence and wait. I could sense the Spirit doing something—draining the pain that was in my soul as the tears came, replenishing the love that had been robbed by people who had treated me in graceless, loveless ways. Eventually, my soul emerged through that stormy season, and I came out without bitterness, without animosity, without accumulated hate or hurt or hopelessness in my soul—because I had been with the Comforter. I didn't come begging Him to do anything; I simply came to Him and drew upon his strength by waiting on Him in silence.

He is a Comforter, and He does comfort those who come and wait upon Him, those who learn to draw upon his strength. You don't have to strive; you don't have to perform. You don't have to fix; you don't have to control outcomes. But you do need to come, with empty hands and an open heart, to the One who heals. The thing God most needs from us to do his work in us is access. He wants access to our hearts and our wills so that He can do a deep work and form Christ in us, and forge the deep faith we need for victory.

It wasn't that the strength would come all at once. The strength would come one day at a time, and it was just enough for that day. The next day I would come again, and He would give me what I needed for the moment. This moment by moment, day by day dependence was just what I needed to learn how to trust Him through the deepest valleys. Trust doesn't come all at once; it is built layer upon layer, moment upon moment. We experience God's faithfulness today, and we learn to trust God a little more tomorrow. This day by day dependence

> When we come in times of pain, He drains us of our self-life and fills us with Himself. We discover that He is what our hearts most need and long for, and we learn to trust Him because He is enough.

solidified my trust in a good Father, and I learned to draw from the resources of his strength in my ever-present weakness and frailty.

So often we come for God to fix us, to make it all better, to take it all away . . . but He simply wants relationship. God isn't interested in fixing us; He wants relationship with us founded on deep trust. This can only be formed in the crucible of time and trials. We often value our comfort and convenience over our character development and God's Kingdom expansion. It is small-minded, shortsighted, and fainthearted. It is only when we take a longer view that we are willing to pay the price necessary to reap the greater reward. We make it too much about us and too little about Him. When we come in times of pain, He drains us of our self-life and fills us with Himself. We discover that He is what our hearts most need and long for, and we learn to trust Him because He is enough.

We need to draw strength from the Spirit as a source of courage. He isn't nervous, He isn't afraid. He isn't uncertain about the future nor anxious about the outcomes. This doesn't mean, this side of Heaven, the outcomes are always going to come out the way we want. They most certainly won't. But his perspective is eternal, not temporal; his peace is heavenly, not earthly. He sits upon his throne in Heaven with peaceful assurance, and He can impart his courage to us in the worst of times, when we need it most, no matter what the outcome may be on this broken planet.

There were times during that season of testing I wanted to quit. But I wouldn't quit because I didn't feel released from God, and I refused to make a decision in the valleys of life, because valley decisions are most always poor decisions. But there were times I was so weary I just didn't feel like I had the strength to go on. When I felt weak, I often received prayer from people who walked with the Spirit, and the Spirit would come and strengthen me. I never had any dramatic encounters when people prayed for me, but there was the comfort of human love and support, there was the clear sense of the Spirit's presence, and I would leave those sessions with greater resolve and courage—honestly, just enough for the day at hand. Jesus taught us to pray, "Give us this day our daily bread," but we often want a year's supply of bread, of strength, of courage, of peace. But we don't learn to trust Him when he supplies in abundance as much as when He supplies just enough for today. Then we have to come back tomorrow for tomorrow's supply. As we come each day and discover He is faithful to supply our daily need, we learn to trust Him for today, for tomorrow, for our future, and for our eternity. I believe there are some things in all our lives that God will not supply for us in abundance—just enough for today, so we will learn to trust Him one day at a time.

Often during times of weakness, I would get away to the monastery for an overnight, and most of those times I took a couple of other men with me. Quite regularly three retired men joined me there: my dad, Bill Westman, and Bo McIntyre, who wrote the book *The Long Journey Home*. We would laugh together, pray together, share together, and spend time alone with God while we were there together. The Spirit used those guys—our laughter, our tears, our sharing, and our prayers— to strengthen me.

Often at the monastery I would get away and walk and worship and enjoy nature. I would enter the time beat up and return home refreshed, strengthened, and renewed, ready for another day of battle against the gates of hell. I could not have made it through the darkest seasons of my life without the Spirit's strength imparted to me. These times alone with God, away on retreat with God and others, often led to new revelations, fresh encounters, renewed strength, and a quickening sense of the Spirit's presence.

I have had so many soul-strengthening, faith-fortifying experiences with God at the monastery that the place has become sacred ground to me. These times deepened my intimacy with the Spirit and developed my confidence in Him. So much of deep faith is developed through a growing intimacy with God that can only come with eager seeking and the passing of well-used time.

We need to draw strength from the Spirit's restorative presence. I learned of the Spirit's restorative presence through meditating on Psalm 23 in a season of angst, which I talk about in *Soul Care*. During that time I sat in silence meditating on this verse from Psalm 23: "He restores my soul" (ESV). In silence, I would access the restorative presence of the Spirit. I could feel the Spirit supplying restoration, peace, and renewal to my inner being. I could feel Him repairing my soul as I waited on Him in silence. Eventually, the anxiety I had been feeling subsided completely, but the lessons I learned have remained with me.

I need to access the restorative presence of God often. The restorative presence of God keeps me calm in times of angst; it restores me in times of depletion; it renews my energy when my inner resources are tapped. The restorative presence of God is like that artesian well of John 7:37 that keeps bubbling up within us, a source of life, a source of refreshing, a source of renewal. It is the eternal life of God available to those who avail themselves to Him in silence and solitude, drawing upon his strength.

I still come regularly just to sit and focus on God's restorative presence. I don't think about anything, or pray anything, or come with any request, or speak any words. I come to sit in his restorative presence, just to be with Him. I find that in his presence I can draw upon his strength. He gives me what I need. He supplies what I lack. He strengthens my weakness. I have found that my words count less than his presence, so I no longer come as much to convey my requests as I come to cultivate his company. In his restorative presence, my soul finds rest and peace, my mind stops racing and trying to find solutions, my heart contents itself with God alone, and my spirit is replenished with his Spirit's abundance. I discover that I have enough; because He is my source, He is enough. In that place of waiting and receiving, I once again am assured that God is for me, not against me, and I am part of an eternal Kingdom with a King who sits on an unchallenged throne with immovable peace. In that secure place, I trust the King.

When I have sat in silence and been in the restorative presence of God, I feel spiritual replenishment and nourishment. It is like air slowly being pumped back into a flat tire. It is like water slowly filling an empty cistern. It is like a sprinkler saturating dry grass so that it comes back to life again. We come with empty hands, and often an emptiness in our soul, but we come to the One who is the very source of life, who has all resources. We wait quietly, and He replenishes us slowly. Most often we do not have a dramatic encounter that cures all, but if we keep coming to Him, over time we discover that the air has somehow been replenished in our soul, the water has been restored to our empty cistern, and our grass is once again green. This is what it is to draw upon the Spirit's strength.

When Jesus departed, He sent us the Spirit so we wouldn't face life alone. On your own, and on my own, we have nothing but empty hands. But with the Spirit, we have all we need for every time, every season, every occasion, every hill, every valley, and every victory, as well as every defeat, every trial and tribulation, and every joy and heartache.

He is with you. And He is all you need. Take time to be with Him and learn to seek Him fervently, wait upon Him patiently, listen to Him obediently, and draw from Him abundantly. He has what it takes.

Reflection Questions

1. In what ways have you experienced the Spirit pouring out the love of the Father in you? Are you currently experiencing the revelation of the Father's love and his delight over you?

2. Are there any blocks preventing you from experiencing the fullness of the Father's love? Do you know what they are? Are you accessing all the resources you need to remove those blocks?

3. How has the Spirit guided you, led you, and spoken to you? How has the Spirit's leading solidified your trust in the Father?

4. Where do you need the Spirit's wisdom and guidance in your current circumstances?

5. When have you experienced the Spirit strengthening you? How have you drawn from his strength?

6. Are you in any circumstance in which you are waiting for abundance and God is offering you only today's supply? Are you gratefully receiving today's supply and trusting Him for each day as it comes?

Conclusion

*"Unbelief is perhaps the most widespread sin
tolerated by Christians today"*

—FRANCIS FRANGIPANE

Since the time I felt the call of God on my life, I knew my purpose was to fight for revival. I had grown up in the church and yet experienced so little—until the day I encountered Jesus as I approached my twentieth year. That day I was overwhelmed with the love of Christ, and my heart was set ablaze for the King and his Kingdom. After that encounter, a passion burned deep within me for all of God's children to be fully surrendered to the lordship of Christ and filled to overflowing with the Spirit. I longed for the church to be the church so the world would believe. My heart ached for renewal, for the church to return to her first love, to the source of supernatural power that marked the church in Acts. I was all in for Jesus and gave my one and only life to this cause that lasts forever.

I expected that revival would come. I thought if I preached on the right topics—like surrender, seeking God, the filling of the Spirit, walking in step with the Spirit, and the mission of Jesus—everyone would come along. I thought everyone would want to surrender if they just understood the fullness of Christ. I was naïve, but I had passion and energy and resolve. I had huge visions fueled by mixed motives. I had great dreams and expectations but shallow faith.

I had to go through a season of purging, refining, trials, and testing for my motives to be purified and my faith developed. The development of faith takes the passing of time and refinement of character. For faith to be forged, it often requires the death, resurrection, and reshaping of an authentic vision from God—as well as severe testing.

> The development of faith takes the passing of time and refinement of character.

This season is simply fraught with danger. It is often in this treacherous season of the "in between"—the time between the promise given and the promise fulfilled—that many God-given dreams are lost. It is during this "in between" season that faith is sometimes not forged, but instead snuffed out—not by God, but by irresolute people who don't process disappointment well. Some people walk away from their faith altogether, but more commonly, people just fail to process deeply, don't press in and press through, and settle for a lesser form of life. They stave off disappointment by expecting little. And they settle for the best the temporal has to offer rather than the passionate dreams of the eternal Kingdom.

Unfulfilled hopes in long seasons of waiting often breed discouragement and disappointment that snuff out our dreams. We take offense at God, and our hearts grow hard, unless we vigilantly process these seasons with an eye toward God's goodness and a heart fully surrendered. But when these trials of faith are faced with the resolve to hold on and give God space to do forming work, warriors emerge wounded but strengthened. Faith is deepened. And certainty is hammered out on the anvil of suffering.

Either the dream would die within me or something within me had to die for the dream to be fulfilled. I processed my disappointments and doubled down on my commitment to pursue God. I became more convinced than ever that I had nothing but empty hands, and that apart from Jesus I could do nothing. I had to search deep and decide if I really believed what the Bible said, or if I would explain away certain portions of Scripture because my experience was anemic and seemed to put the lie to the promise. I chose to go all in for the veracity of Scripture, for the ultimate fulfillment of the promises of Jesus, and for John 14:12: "Very truly I tell you, all who have faith in me will do the works I have been doing, and they will do even greater things than these, because I am going to the Father."

All—not most, not some, not an elite few, but all—"will do the works I have been doing," and even "greater things." Casting out demons, healing the sick, saving the lost, and seeing the captives set free. This was the work Jesus was doing; this is the work of the church. This was the promise of God for my life, and I would not settle for a lesser, watered-down version of it. But the whole promise was contingent on faith: "All who have faith in me."

My God was big enough, but my faith was too small. My passion was strong enough, but my character was too weak. My vision was deep enough, but my intimacy with God was too shallow. God had to do a work in me before He could do the work through me that He wanted to do. To resist the inner work of God is to forfeit the vision of God being fulfilled. My faith had to move down the spectrum, and in some places my faith had shallow roots and was weak, wobbly, and could not sustain all God had in mind. So I let the master teacher come and teach me so the work can be done.

I am so grateful for all the master teacher taught me and

formed in me. I never had anything but empty hands, and a willing spirit, but fortunately for us, that is all He needs, along with the resolve to persevere. Like Peter, I discovered my spirit was often willing but my flesh weak—nevertheless, He saw me through. I am still not seeing everything I want to see, but I am seeing far more than I have ever seen. I have not arrived, and there are still plenty of days where my faith wobbles, but not like it used to. There are areas where my faith remains underdeveloped, but there are other areas where my faith is certain. I'm growing, but it hasn't been an accidental journey.

I was in a class recently where two people were healed even though we didn't pray for their healing! They were healed just sitting in class because of the gracious presence of our healing God. That was fun. They gave testimony, and it encouraged all of us, so we ended up praying for three other people who were sick. We laid hands on them, lingered with them in the presence of God, and came in with eager anticipation given what had just happened to the two in class. But not one of them was healed. Why? I don't know. Was our faith too weak? Was the enemy too strong—not for God, but for us? Is there a sovereign purpose yet to be fulfilled? I don't know. There is plenty of room for mystery in all of this.

But this is what I do know: I know that John 14:12 is true. I know that I am not responsible for God's part of the miraculous workings, but only my part, which is to have faith in Jesus. I know I come to every encounter with empty hands; I cannot make anything happen in the spirit realm. I know I am responsible for developing my faith, strengthening my character, deepening my intimacy, and resolving to pass the tests and trials that come my way without taking offense at God. I know I am seeing more of the works of the Kingdom in my life than ever before. And I know all of it has nothing to do with me. I am simply grateful—moved to tears, actually—humbled, and awestruck that God would choose to partner with the likes of us.

After I emerged from the dark night of the soul, I noticed a difference when I laid hands on people. After that season, when I laid hands on people, with great regularity they experienced God in power. The prayer I had prayed for twenty years was being answered: "Lord, give me the ability to impart your Spirit, if my character and intimacy can sustain it."

I noticed there were certain people that I felt the Spirit of God highlight to me, and I specifically would sense God asking me to pray a prayer of impartation over them. When I followed the leading of the Spirit and prayed for these people, the prayer of impartation that God called me to pray, all of them fell to the ground under the weight of God's presence. None had ever fallen to the ground in a prayer like that before. This wasn't learned behavior; this was simply, and powerfully, God's doing. After those prayers, many times the people would report back to me things that had shifted in their lives. Some of them felt heat when they prayed for others for the first time. Some of them said they experienced a noticeable increase in authority. Others told me they started seeing healings when they prayed for the sick, though they had never seen that before. Still others said they began to see people filled with the Spirit when they prayed for people with the laying on of hands.

At this point, I have felt prompted by God to pray a prayer of impartation for lay people, church leaders, pastors, bishops, district superintendents, denominational leaders, and presidents of denominations or other nonprofit organizations, and God has visited them in these ways. It is all God's work; I remind you that this is the testimony of Jesus, and I have nothing but empty hands. God works in cooperation with our faith. We come with nothing to Him who is able.

Doug came to one of our Soul Care Equipping Conferences, and from the moment I met him I could sense the Spirit's work in his life. He was hungry for God and passionate to see the works of the Kingdom released in his region of the world. He was ready to listen, eager to learn, and quick to absorb all he could.

He came to multiple conferences in which I was speaking, and we shared some meals together. One of the things I loved about Doug was that he wasn't just a learner; he was a practitioner. He took the things we talked about and dove into the deep end of the pool. He took risks and put them into action. He learned about deliverance and went home and started immediately to try and help the captives get free.

During a Soul Care conference he attended, I gave a talk on the baptism of the Spirit. I asked all those who wanted more of the presence and power of God in their life to stand, and I asked the people who were walking in the fullness of the Spirit to pray for those who wanted more. Doug and his group? Every one of them stood. I made a beeline right for them because I sensed God wanted me to pray for them. I laid hands on Doug first, and simply said, "Now come, Holy Spirit. Freely I have received, freely I give. That which you have given to me, this longing to fight for revival, I impart to him."

Before I finished the prayer, Doug was falling over under the presence of God. I prayed for the rest of the group that was with him, and they all fell beside him, one by one. Later Doug told me that they went and prayed with each other that night, and for the first time in their lives, when they prayed, they felt heat in their hands. They went back to their place in the world and held a conference for the things of the Spirit. The first conference they held after that prayer time they saw healings like never before. Two people were healed who had multiple sclerosis and were in wheelchairs. They rolled in on their wheelchairs and walked out under their own strength because of the power of Jesus. They saw a blind person receive sight. These leaders weren't even the ones who prayed for the people who experienced these miracles; they were simply the ones who created the atmosphere where the works of the Kingdom could be manifest. Jesus is the healer; Jesus gets the glory. Only Jesus.

Jesus wants to advance his Kingdom. He wants us to do the works of the Kingdom, even greater things than these. This is the promise of Jesus for all who have faith in Him. But the faith that moves the hands of Jesus to release the works of the Kingdom is a faith that is developed.

It is a faith that moves from hope to expectation to certainty. It is a faith that is developed through intimacy and with intentionality. It is a faith that is forged through trials and testing with long periods of persistent waiting. It is a faith that is shaped and refined by our response to the work of the Spirit. It is a faith that is cultivated in a heart of humility. It is a faith that is needed in the world today.

Certain faith won't be developed in passivity or formed in ease. But it can be developed, it can be formed, and it is worth all that we must pay for it. Jesus is worth it. Imagine living your life with such certain faith that when you get to Heaven, Jesus tells you He was amazed by your great faith. That is a noble life, one worth aspiring to. May the halls of Heaven resound with the testimony of Jesus because our generation has cultivated such deep faith!

ABOUT THE AUTHOR

Rev. Dr. Rob Reimer was the Founding and Lead Pastor of South Shore Community Church, a church of the Christian and Missionary Alliance in Brockton, Massachusetts until June of 2017 when he followed the call of God to become a full time professor at Alliance Theological Seminary in New York. Under Rob's leadership, what began as a small group of eight believers mobilized on a mission to start a new church, resulting in hundreds of people coming to faith in Christ. Many of the examples and stories from his books come from the lessons learned from planting and leading a church in New England—one of the most unchurched regions in the nation.

In addition to his role as Lead Pastor, Rob is also an accomplished author. His books, *Pathways to the King, River Dwellers*, and *Soul Care*, have been sold worldwide.

A gifted preacher and communicator, Rob preached weekly at South Shore Community and is a sought-after speaker. He regularly speaks at conferences, leadership retreats, mission fields, churches, and seminaries in the United States and abroad. His sermons are posted online and accessed by people around the world.

Rob is also an experienced teacher. He is currently a full time Professor of Pastoral Theology at Alliance Theological Seminary (ATS) in Nyack, New York, where he had taught as an adjunct for 15 years. He teaches Soul Care at the doctoral level and has taught various classes at the masters level, including Personal, Professional and Theological Foundations for Ministry; Evangelism; Mentoring; Pastoral Methods; Person in Ministry; Soul Care; and Intimacy and Authority.

Rob was ordained as a Minister of the Gospel of Jesus Christ by the Christian and Missionary Alliance in 1993. He earned a bachelor's degree in English from King's College, a Master's of Divinity from Alliance Theological Seminary, and a Doctorate in Preaching from Gordon-Conwell Theological Seminary.

Rob and his wife, Jen, have four children, Danielle, Courtney, Darcy, and Craig.

To learn more, visit www.DrRobReimer.com

ALSO BY ROB REIMER

Soul Care: 7 Transformational Principles for a Healthy Soul

Brokenness grasps for the soul of humanity. We are broken body, soul, and spirit, and we need the healing touch of Jesus. Soul Care explores seven principles that are profound healing tools of God: securing your identity, repentance, breaking family sin patterns, forgiving others, healing wounds, overcoming fears, and deliverance.

Dr. Reimer challenges readers to engage in an interactive, roll-up-your-sleeves and get messy process—a journey of self-reflection, Holy Spirit inspiration, deep wrestling, and surrender. It is a process of discovering yourself in true community and discovering God as He pierces through the layers of your heart.

Life change is hard. But these principles, when packaged together and lived out, can lead to lasting transformation, freedom, and a healthy soul. Soul Care encourages you to gather a small group of comrades in arms, read and process together, open your souls to one another, access the presence and power of God together, and journey into the freedom and fullness of Christ.

Soul Care DVD Teaching Series

Rob's first video teaching series is an in-depth guide to Soul Care. Great for individuals, small groups, or church-wide curriculum, this series will be an invaluable guide to anyone who is going after freedom and fullness in Christ, or endeavoring to lead others along that journey.

River Dwellers: Living in the Fullness of the Spirit

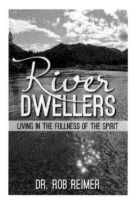

Have you ever wished there was more to your Christian life? Too often the Christian life is reduced to going to church, attending meetings, serving God, and doing devotions. But Jesus promised us abundant life—a deep, intimate, satisfying connection with the living God. How do we access the abundant life that Jesus promised? The key is the presence and life of the Holy Spirit within us.

Jesus said that the Spirit of God flows within us like a river; He is the River of Life. But we need to dwell in the river in order to access the Spirit's fullness.

In this book, Dr. Reimer offers a deep look at life in the Spirit and provides practical strategies for dwelling in the River of Life. Rob explores the fullness of the Spirit, tuning in to the promptings of the Spirit, walking in step with the Spirit, and developing sensitivity to the presence of the God in our lives. This resource will guide you toward becoming a full-time river dweller, even during life's most difficult seasons, when the river seems to run low.

Pathways to the King: Living a Life of Fullness and Power

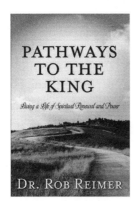

We need revival. The church in America desperately needs revival. There are pockets of it happening, but we need another Great Awakening. About forty years ago, the church was impacted by the church growth movement. The goal of the movement was to get the church focused on the Great Commission—taking the Good News about Jesus to the entire world. The church was off mission, and the movement was a necessary course correction. But it didn't work. Many people came to Christ as a result of this outreach emphasis, and we can be grateful for that. More churches are now focused on evangelism, helping people come to know Jesus, than they were before the movement. But we have fewer people (by percentage) attending church now than ever before in the history of the United States. We need revival.

This book is about how we can usher in revival and about the price we must pay to experience it. Dr. Reimer believes we have a part to play in seeing the next great spiritual awakening. God wants us to be carriers of His kingdom. He wants us to experience the reality and fullness of His kingdom, and he wants us to expand the kingdom to others, just like Jesus did. To do that, we must follow eight Kingdom Pathways of Spiritual Renewal: Personalizing our Identity in Christ, Pursuing God, Purifying Ourselves, Praising, Praying

Kingdom Prayers, Claiming Promises, Passing the Tests, and Persisting. These eight pathways are discussed in great detail, are securely rooted in biblical truths, and are illustrated by compelling examples from Scripture and from Dr. Reimer's life, the lives of believers in his community, and in the lives of great Christians throughout history.